T0322661

THE DIARY OF A
HURRICANE
PILOT
IN THE BATTLE OF FRANCE
FRANCIS BLACKADDER OF 607 SQUADRON

THE DIARY OF A
HURRICANE
PILOT

IN THE BATTLE OF FRANCE

FRANCIS BLACKADDER OF 607 SQUADRON

ROBERT DIXON

FONTHILL

Blackadder in a Spitfire, 1944.

Page 2: No. 607 Squadron, 1938. Detail taken from picture on page 27.

Fonthill Media Limited
Fonthill Media LLC
www.fonthillmedia.com
office@fonthillmedia.com

First published in the United Kingdom
and the United States of America 2015

British Library Cataloguing in Publication Data:
A catalogue record for this book is available from the British Library

ISBN 978-1-78155-310-7

Typeset in 10.5pt on 13pt Sabon
Printed and bound by CPI Group (UK) Ltd, Croydon, CR0 4YY

Contents

Blackadder at the Air Fighting Development Squadron, May 1945.

Acknowledgements

A project such as this requires a great deal of help. I would firstly like to thank Robert Blackadder and the Blackadder family for their cooperation, encouragement, and hospitality. The subject is after all a private document, and permission to access the writings as well as photographs of Francis Blackadder was very gratefully received.

Mr Nicholas Craig was also a great help, as he always has been in the past; so has Charles J. Sample, who laid his family photograph albums as well as papers open to inspection. Both these men were willing to answer the most awkward of questions.

I would also like to acknowledge the help given by the late Pamela Turner, who let me delve into the logbooks of her late husband, Group Captain W. H. N. (Willy) Turner, and the support and hospitality of the Turner family. Mrs Davinia Helps also deserves a special mention for providing information on her cousin Launcelot Eustice Smith, and her father Doctor David Smith (Doc Dave). I would also like to thank Jen Main of the archive office of Merchiston School.

I give special thanks to Miranda M. White, who went beyond the call of duty in supplying copies of her father James Michael Bazin's logbooks; to Mrs Rosemary Gaskell who provided copies of her father Peter Parrott's logbooks; and especially to Hugh Gore, for photographs and information of his uncle Will Gore. Mr Ian Pearce deserves mention for his great help in supplying the logbooks of George Morley Fidler.

The CWGC deserves praise, as does the RAF Historical Branch and the Bundesarchiv in Berlin and Aachen. The information from Jacquelin Cox of the Cambridge University Archives also warrants special credit; local newspapers, such as the *Northern Echo*, *Sunderland Echo*, and *Newcastle Journal*; and various cemeteries and crematoria, ever overlooked when thanks are given out. No matter how small the contribution, I thank you all. For the endless supplies of nutrition over a long period—I would like to thank my wife Shirley.

The watch office, Vitry: Parrott, Thompson, Dixon, Pumphrey, Blackadder, Gore, and Smith standing by the door (from left to right). Detail taken from picture on page 50.

Foreword

In common, I suspect, with many of the post-war generation of this country, whose families and relatives had participated in service action during the Second World War, I knew until only very recently precious little of substance about the subject of this account, namely my own father, William Francis Blackadder's involvement. This ignorance I attribute in retrospect to two factors: firstly, a totally understandable reluctance on his part to relive the most traumatic, life-changing experience imaginable and one impossible to convey to any who had not themselves participated in this critical watershed in our history; and secondly, an endearing modesty bordering on reticence, prevalent among many of his fellow fighters, who can in fact claim to personify the true heroes of that time.

Much has been written elsewhere on the Battle of Britain's pivotal role in 1940 in helping to preserve our island's freedom from invasion, which in turn created the only viable platform for the successful launch of Operation Overlord on D-Day to liberate Europe for years later. Far less, I feel, has been chronicled of its predecessor, the Battle for France of 1939–40, so the publication here in full, for the first time, of my father's actual handwritten diary of that campaign will, I am confident, help fill a gap in our knowledge.

Robert Dixon is already a well-known contributor in this field, having earlier written a full account of my father's Auxiliary Air Force Squadron in his publication, *No. 607 Squadron: A Shade of Blue*, as well as numerous related articles on the period in question. In this latest work, his well-informed introduction covers the background to my father from his schooling in Edinburgh and pre-war air training right up to the moment when No. 607 Squadron was called to arms in August 1940. This is followed by a verbatim transcription of my father's personal diary, 'A'

Flight 607 (Fighter) Squadron Auxiliary Air Force: Usworth 12/8/39–4/6/40, reflecting the eight-month Phony War period and culminating in the critical days of May 1940 when the Germans appeared invincible and Britain faced the gravest crisis in her history. Robert Dixon's account concludes with his own interpretation, supported by my father's pilot log books of the latter's own as well as the squadron's involvement during those momentous days and weeks of the Battle of Britain from July to October 1940, and followed by his later transfer to a series of non-flying posts during the remainder of the war and subsequently.

I am delighted to be given this opportunity to record my own family's gratitude to Robert Dixon for the painstaking time and effort he has invested in this long-awaited record of someone very close to us, who nevertheless chose not to divulge his true contribution to the national cause in his lifetime. He himself would have elected not to have had his story published, believing to the end that his contemporaries were only carrying out their fundamental duty in fighting for the future freedom of this country. This understandable viewpoint, however, must be outweighed by the increasing necessity to maintain for future generations the memory of the sacrifices made by our servicemen and women, to preserve for this country and the rest of the free world the liberty which we still enjoy today.

Robert H. Blackadder
December 2013, Shoreham by Sea, West Sussex

Introduction

This is a book featuring one man's diary—the diary of a pilot. It covers the period from the heady beginnings of the Second World War in 1939 to British defeat in the Battle of France. Although the book covers this battle in some detail, it is not a blow by blow account. Neither is it a definitive account, a feat unlikely to be achieved due to the amount of research still in progress in that field.

The pilot, William Francis Blackadder (known as 'Francis') was a member of a band known as the 'part-timers', or even the 'long-haired boys'—the pilots of the Auxiliary Air Force.

The diary begins in a light-hearted vein, although the country was preparing for a war. Blackadder's diary takes us through its outbreak, and the hustle and bustle of waiting and patrolling for the enemy's delayed appearance. Blackadder's entries become increasingly cheerful at the prospect of—at last—going to France. It would be a great adventure, and was not predicted to last beyond Christmas.

Although the diary was initially intended as an *aide mémoire*, the imminent mobilisation to France brings other pilots into the story. They party, go to all the 'top shows' and even venture into Paris. Endless rain and snow causes them havoc in the winter, but the pilots' spirits are not dampened. Engines initially refuse to start, and when they eventually do, the aircraft have difficulty in taking off, so bogged down are they in the deep snow. Yet still, Blackadder treats the French campaign as some kind of fun romp. It is only when the promise of Hawker Hurricanes continually fails to materialise that the pilots do become frustrated. Where are they? When will we get them?

Of course, the 'part-timers' ultimately do get their much-needed Hurricanes. We accompany Blackadder on the few short weeks of the

Blitzkrieg after Germany launches its attack on 10 May 1940. The diary at this point changes tone, its tempo accelerates—gone is the 'Phoney War'. Unlike other reports, it is written on a day-to-day basis as events unfold. We feel fear and excitement as Blackadder flies over a river at zero feet; the trees above us, as he evades the pursuing enemy; his despair, when he resorts to tears after a hectic patrol.

As the battle rages on, Blackadder is forced to fight on the run. He moves from one airfield to the next, sometimes with nowhere to sleep in between, as piece after piece of France falls to the all-conquering Luftwaffe. Finally, retreat is made to England in desolation. The RAF have faced their first battle, and lost.

The war will not be over soon, but will be drawn out into a long affair. Blackadder has entered the war as an inexperienced young man, but by the end of the Battle of France, emerges as a seasoned and battle-hardened fighter pilot. His job now is to pass on his knowledge to the many more inexperienced pilots who will take on the Luftwaffe.

1

Beginnings

The Blackadder family has its immediate origins in the county of Berwickshire, on the Scottish side of the Anglo-Scottish border. This was part of the area known in the past for its lawlessness and its fighting men. Robert Blackadder was an architect's apprentice and lived in Ninewells Mains Farm to the west of Chirnside. The family are traceable to farmers in the Blanerne area, well into the nineteenth century. Nearby is a hamlet named Blackadder, as well as the River Blackadder, which meanders into the River Tweed. At a later date, Robert Blackadder took up residence in Grange Road, Edinburgh, probably in search of architectural employment. Later still, he married Francis Gwendaline Boddy, and the couple set up home in Edinburgh. They had three sons between 1908 and 1913: John Hew Patrick, Robert Prendergast, and William Francis.

From 1926 to 1930, the youngest, William Francis, attended Merchiston Castle School, an independent boarding school for boys within a couple of miles of Edinburgh's city centre.[1] Originally, the school building had been owned by John Napier, the inventor of logarithms. The school had a strong rugby tradition and was only a short distance away from Murrayfield stadium. Blackadder moved from Merchiston to study at Edinburgh University from 1930 to 1931, after which he immediately took up further study in Modern Languages and History at Gonville and Caius College, Cambridge, until 1935.

With his studies completed, Blackadder found employment with the Runciman shipping line based in Newcastle upon Tyne in 1936. He seems to have manifested little interest in aviation prior to this period, and it may originally have come from Leslie Runciman, also a Cambridge graduate. Runciman was a keen pilot, and had his own aircraft; he often flew to the Continent, and on one occasion flew his Gypsy Moth to a political

William Francis Blackadder in his early rugby days.

Leslie Runciman.

meeting in support of his mother, a Liberal candidate. He had also had some success in the Kings Cup Air Races, achieving third place in 1933. In 1930, he became Commanding Officer (CO) of the newly formed No. 607 (County of Durham) Squadron, AAF.[2]

What about the Auxiliary Air Force, still in its infant stages, attracted the young, recently graduated Blackadder to its ranks? Nothing appears to have been written in answer to this question; only records of his movements and employment during the period can give us some idea of his motivations. Joining this territorial unit out of a sense of national pride or duty to the common good does not appear to have been a factor. It is far more likely that Blackadder perceived aviation as a means of improving his social standing, or simply as another career path. After all, it was employment at the Runciman Shipping Line that first brought him to the north-east.

The emerging Auxiliary Air Force (AAF) was the brainchild of Sir Hugh Montague Trenchard—made Viscount in 1936—who fought long and hard to bring his idea to fruition. He envisaged the auxiliary force in bases all over the world, fuelled by the territorial rather than the patriotic loyalty of its members—an approach not dissimilar to the Territorial Army's. Rather than simply rallying to a distant power in times of hostility, recruits would be defending their own land or county. Trenchard also pictured his new force as part of the RAF, but not as a supplement to it. Not to be looked on as a mere back-up to the 'full-timers', the AAF would be at their vanguard, and have its own design—as Trenchard saw it, 'The Royal Yacht Squadron of the RAF', or, in another age, a crack cavalry unit. Originally, AAF COs came from the RAF, but this soon changed, as did their commission, from full- to part-time membership. The AAF gradually distanced itself from the regular RAF, with the single concession that each squadron had to have two permanent RAF liaison officers on its staff. These two officers also doubled up as adjutants, assistants, and flying instructors on the squadron.

Trenchard also planned to fill the AAF with the progeny of the social elite—young men whose heritage had already instilled in them an instinct for leadership. Their fathers would be land-owners, high-ranking members of the establishment, and, in many cases, military leaders of the previous generation. In addition, the AAF would make the University Air Squadrons its stomping ground. Social connections were part and parcel of life on an AAF squadron, and Leslie Runciman's appointment to CO of No. 607 Squadron proved no exception. He was not only the heir to the Runciman Shipping Line, but the eldest son of the first Viscount Runciman of Doxford (created in 1937), a lawyer and Liberal MP in Asquith's government, and Hilda Runciman, liberal MP for St Ives.

Leslie had attended Eton, like his father, before moving on to becoming a King's Scholar at Trinity College, Cambridge—an education shared by most if not all of the pilots on No. 607 Squadron. In other words, these young men came from a specific social background, one that would in fact exclude many would-be pilots from contention.

Unsurprisingly, Cambridge University had a strong connection with No. 607 Squadron. Apart from Runciman, Launcelot Smith went to Cambridge after attending Marlborough School, and later became a director in his family's shipping business (Smiths Dock). Also graduated from Cambridge were Will Gore, Peter Dixon, Dudley Craig, Monty Thompson, and Francis Blackadder. Though a small number held positions in family businesses, land management, and the stock exchange, No. 607 Squadron officers were roughly divided into those who held positions in engineering—mechanical, electrical, and marine—and those who were in the law profession. Many of their fathers, grandfathers, and even great-grandfathers had passed through the same public schools, universities, and professions, which meant that AAF pilots often knew each other personally. The web of connections linking pilots from one squadron to another encouraged a feeling of territorial and social kinship. These men were not only predestined to lead, but to do so from within their own county's auxiliary unit.

Pumphrey, Humpherson, and Smith (from left to right).

This is not to say that all pilots were academically brilliant. Public schools and universities were simply an advantageous formality for pilot candidates of an auxiliary squadron. Academic success, on the other hand, was not a prerequisite; attendance alone was a sufficient recommendation. Monty Thompson, for instance, the son of a Newcastle lawyer, attended Hayleybury School and studied Law at Cambridge, but only achieved a third class in early examinations. He later failed to attain honours, and graduated by proxy on 21 June 1938; he did not bother to attend the awards ceremony.

Although Runciman was initially 'picky' in his choice of pilots, this changed at the end of 1937. He wrote that he was 'anxious during the next few months to take on a rather larger entry than normal', and began to send letters to the managers of various industrial firms—the source of many existing pilots on the squadron—asking them to place adverts for No. 607 Squadron. He asked the managers to encourage 'men of the right calibre' to come along, meet No. 607 Squadron, and see what they could be doing with their spare time.[3] However, the days in which the AAF provided a training route for pilots were numbered: it came into competition with the Royal Air Force Volunteer Reserve (RAFVR), to whom it had offered training. The RAFVR grew more popular as a result of this initiative, by virtue of enabling the common man to access AAF training without having to meet its exclusive social requirements.

Normally, admission to the auxiliary squadrons proceeded by letter or introduction via a member of the squadron, followed by an invitation to visit the base. In the case of Francis Blackadder, this would probably have been done by Runciman himself, since they were both personally and professionally acquainted. Blackadder applied to join No. 607 Squadron either in the latter half of 1935, or in early 1936.

After dinner with the commanding officer and his wife, the next step was a flight in one of the squadron's aircraft, accompanied by a flying instructor. Blackadder's first flight is recorded in his logbook to have taken place on a Saturday afternoon, 19 January 1936, in Avro K2387. The flying instructor on record was Flt Lt Singer, and the flight itself lasted some thirty minutes, going up to 2,000 feet. Blackadder noted in his new logbook that this was a 'suitability' flight. A few slight turns may have been included, since the point of the exercise was to establish whether the candidate had the right temperament and did not suffer from air-sickness.

Of course, procedures were altered over the years. Harry Welford was one of the later pilots to join No. 607 Squadron; originally from London, he moved north to attend Armstrong College—now Newcastle University—as well as Durham University, where he studied Engineering. He resided with his cousin, Bobby Pumphrey, in Sunderland, and when

Welford mentioned that he would like to do something along the auxiliary line—though he never mentioned aviation—Pumphrey suggested that he apply to No. 607 Squadron. A flight was arranged with Pumphrey as pilot, which went well, until Pumphrey decided to enter a loop—not a wise choice for a pilot candidate on his first flight. Upon landing, Welford paid for the results and was promptly sick over the side of the plane. A passing officer gave Pumphrey a tongue-lashing for carrying out aerobatics on a candidate test flight, and ordered him to clean up the mess. However, it did Welford no harm, as his simple diary entry on 4 December 1938 indicates: '[...] had been accepted for training'.

Blackadder's second flight took place on Wednesday 23 January, once more with Flt Lt Singer, and in the same aircraft. This was another local flight, lasting thirty-five minutes, and going up to 2,000 feet. The fact that this took place on a weekday afternoon seems to confirm the theory that pilots of the AAF were in employment that made allowances for time off. On this occasion, Blackadder refers to himself as a 'prospective candidate'.

Usworth, 1940: Lenahan, ??, Welford, and Bowen (from left to right).

It may have taken three weeks to come to a decision regarding his flying career, or it may have been difficult for Blackadder to secure more time off from work. In any case, he did not fly again or begin his training in earnest until 15 March 1936. This consisted of a forty-minute flight, up to 2,000 feet in Avro K2387, and again with Flt Lt Singer as the flying instructor. Most of Blackadder's training was carried out on weekends, with the odd flight on a Thursday.[4]

It was on Sunday 17 May that Blackadder made his most memorable flight. After the usual trip with Singer, Blackadder was sent up on his first solo exercise in Avro K1806: this lasted five minutes and only took him up to 1,000 feet, but was nevertheless an exhilarating experience. He repeated the same exercise on 25 May, followed by a flight of fifty-five minutes: Blackadder was now a pilot. Because No. 607 was still a bomber squadron during this period, Blackadder was given a flight in one of the squadrons' Wapitis on the very same day by CO Leslie Runciman. However, the conversion into a fighter squadron was not far off.

The highlight of any auxiliary airman's career—whether they were a pilot or member of ground crew—was the annual summer camp. This was part-time training turned into reality, for on this occasion, the AAF got a chance to partake in the life and work of their full-time counterparts. All summer camps were set up at various RAF airfields and focused on the flying programme elaborated by the CO and his commanders. Leslie Runciman was well-known for making every one of his men count within the squadron: 'Every man had to feel he had a purpose on the squadron, rather than just turning up'.[5] In 1936, the summer camp was held at RAF Tangmere in West Sussex.

Blackadder had been gazetted as a pilot officer on 1 June 1936; on 3 July, he was off to his first summer camp. Blackadder flew solo—normally a passenger was carried—to Tangmere in Avro K2864 by way of Catterick, Hucknall, and Bicester. Poor visibility set in over the south, and Blackadder was obliged to make a landing at Farnborough before continuing to Tangmere. Blackadder flew both as a trainer pilot and as a passenger at summer camp. Tangmere also gave Blackadder a taste of the Hawker Hart, a training biplane, because the squadron was to be transferred to Fighter Command and re-equipped with the real combat Hawker Demon by the end of September that year.

Blackadder's first Hart was the K6488, in which he flew as a passenger with his flying instructor Flt Lt Singer. When the summer camp ended, Blackadder flew home to Usworth on 17 July as a passenger of the Hart K3961, piloted by Joe Kayll; this gave Blackadder a little more experience of the Hawker Hart. From this time onwards, he did most of his training with Flt Lt Graham Ashley Leonard 'Minnie' Manton, who had taken

No. 607 Squadron Avro Tutor, Usworth.

over from Flt Lt Singer. Blackadder flew solo on 1 November in the Hart K3861. However, his real breakthrough came at the end of the month, when he flew a Hawker Demon K5686 solo for the first time—he could now call himself a fighter pilot.

Switching to the Demon created a few problems, one of which was the squadron motto—now that No. 607 had become a fighter unit, it had to have one. Some strange suggestions were made, but the phrase to ultimately become No. 607's creed was 'UP'. Runciman and the College of Heralds exchanged correspondence on the matter: the college could not sanction 'UP', but proposed 'Upwards' instead. Runciman replied that this was not good enough; it had to be 'UP', because of its resonance with an obscure joke shared by his pilots. However, the College's answer remained 'no'![6] When the squadron did eventually join Fighter Command, it had to carry its spearhead on the tail of its aircraft, and the squadron crest within it. Fighter Command deemed that the spearhead should point forwards, so all the photographs of No. 607 Squadron's Demons from this time show the spearhead pointing 'UP'! In a way, No. 607 Squadron had earned its motto, unofficially or not.

1937 held highs and lows in store for Blackadder. It started off quietly, with a number of cross-country flights in January carried out with either Flt Lts Bartlett or Manton. He did, however, carry out three solo flights in the Demon on 4 February, as he was beginning to gain confidence and

Tail of a Demon showing No. 607's 'UP' device.

experience of the new aircraft. Everything went well until 28 March, when Blackadder attempted a solo cross-country flight at 3,000 feet, from Falstone to Wooler, in Demon K5689. It should be noted that Wooler lies at the northernmost tip of the Cheviot Hills, and that its high ground and bad weather made it a local danger spot and graveyard of aircraft. Blackadder's flight was indeed disrupted by low cloud and rain, but he was able to turn back and flew to Falstone. Upon landing, however, he made a misjudgement and 'overran' the airfield; he then attempted to bring the Demon to a halt, but leaned too heavily on the brakes, with the result that the Demon tipped onto its nose. This was not to be the last embarrassment of his career.

Not discouraged, Blackadder continued with his training. He recorded his first passenger-carrying flight in Demon K5687. The passenger, listed in his logbook as 'Newman', may well have been a new recruit to the squadron, possibly making his first flight. Passengers normally had their names entered into Blackadder's logbook, whether they were air-gunners or simply along for the ride; the only exception appears to have been an un-named person entered as 'ballast'!

There was a fatal accident on 14 May: Tim Richardson, on the return leg of a cross-country flight from Sutton Bridge, was caught out by the low-lying mist off the Durham coast. His Demon crashed onto the beach at Dawdon and he did not survive. Richardson was a fairly recent addition to the squadron, and a contemporary of Blackadder's, so this would doubtless have had some effect on Blackadder, who was not flying on the day of the accident, and unlike other pilots, did not comment on the incident in his logbook.

Blackadder was singled out for duties in the coronation of King George VI in London on 10 May. He was put in charge of two NCOs and eight airmen to provide street-lining on Constitution Hill, and was awarded the Coronation Medal for his part in the festivities. Nine days later, the squadron was rechristened, from 'No. 6 Auxiliary Group' to '12 Fighter Group', a fully-fledged fighter squadron. The only thing not to change was the three-flight system, which became two flights at a later date.

Instrument and formation flying were to be the mainstay of Blackadder's training during this period. Instrument flying was practised in the Avro Tutor with John Sample on one occasion, and Tim Carr-Ellison on another. The highlight of the year came on 8 August, when the full squadron flew from Usworth to Newtonards, then on to Mount Stewart, and were the luncheon guests of Lord Londonderry, Honorary Commander of No. 607 Squadron. Blackadder flew as a passenger in Demon K5692 piloted by Carr-Ellison.

Just a week later, the squadron departed for its annual summer camp, that year to be held at Rochford. Blackadder flew there in Demon K5692 with Leading Aircraftman (LAC) Armstrong in the back seat; the flight went smoothly until the landing, which was once again too heavy, and caused the undercarriage to break. The Demon tipped up onto its nose, additionally damaging the lower starboard wing tip.[7] A photograph taken on the day shows a group of airmen watching as LAC Armstrong unloads his baggage from the rear cockpit. Blackadder does not log the event, and neither does it feature in the squadron Operations Record Book (ORB). This seems out of character, in that Blackadder never shied away from accepting responsibility for his accidents.

In the 1937 summer camp, the whole squadron was billeted under canvas and aircraft were picketed to simulate war conditions. Blackadder spent much time on a mixture of formation and cross-country flights; he also carried out low-level dive-bombing at Eastchurch as part of a simulation. One flight of interest was a 15,000-feet battle-climb, achieved in Demon K5683; the man in the back seat was listed as 'AC English'— Charles Edward English. After training as a fighter pilot, English would go on to fly many operations with No. 85 Squadron in the Battle of Britain.[8]

When the squadron became part of Fighter Command, much emphasis was placed on night flying training. This began at the 1937 summer camp and intensified after No. 607 Squadron's return to Usworth. Blackadder recorded many dual night flights with Flt Lt Manton. Meanwhile, Runciman attempted to secure more aircraft for the squadron, as much

Lord Londonderry.

Blackadder's crash at Rochford, 1937.

of his correspondence with Leigh-Mallory reveals. 'The squadron needed a Hawker Hart to replace the ageing Avro 504', wrote Runciman, '…this aircraft is no longer any use to us.' Leigh-Mallory took on board Runciman's request, and responded that they would soon get a number of Demons, in addition to a Hart.[9]

At the end of November, Blackadder's flying days were temporarily drawn to halt on account of his work commitments. His last flight for a while was a battle-climb in Demon K5693. Still an employee of the Runciman Shipping Line, Blackadder was sent to work in their Glasgow office: this was too far from Usworth for training, but the posting would not last long enough to warrant transferring to another squadron.[10] On the other hand, the move to Glasgow did enable him to pour more energy into his rugby training: he became a member of the first Scottish team to beat England, at Twickenham on 19 March 1938. He returned to Usworth in April.

The AAF squadrons competed for the Esher Trophy on the basis of their combat efficiency, and on 12 February 1938, it was fought for at Usworth. No. 607 Squadron—the squadron chosen to represent 12 Group—came second to No. 604 (County of Middlesex) Squadron by seventeen points. The pilots representing No. 607 Squadron were Smith, Vick, Sample, Kayll, Bazin, and Pumphrey. John Hawkes, Francis Blackadder, and the 'mainly' regular air-gunner Charles Edward English were enrolled as reserves. These were the names listed in Leslie Runciman's private papers, which must have been made earlier on in the year, because Blackadder was away from the squadron from 29 October 1937 to 10 April 1938, and therefore not available to fly. Neither, as it happens, was Jim Bazin available on the 12th, and he makes no mention of the Esher Trophy in his logbook. There must, therefore, have been a later change to Runciman's selection.

Upon returning to No. 607 Squadron, Blackadder's first exercise was a dual-flight with the new flying instructor, Flt Lt William Henry Nigel (Willy) Turner, carried out in Hart K6482 on 10 April 1938.[11] This was meant to give him a brush up, and he followed it up with a flight in Demon K5684, on which he noted the 'ballast' passenger in the back seat. The point of the Demon K5684 flight was training with oxygen equipment, and it went up to 26,000 feet.

Meanwhile, all was not well on the ground. Runciman questioned whether Usworth was the best place to be for No. 607 Squadron, because underground workings from the local coal mines were leaving the airfield increasingly liable to subsidence. He also voiced concern to Leigh-Mallory that the airfield suffered from industrial haze and coastal fog, given its proximity to the sea. Runciman was no doubt thinking of the death of Tim

Blackadder, third from the rear left, Tangmere.

W. H. N. Willy Turner in his
Cranwell days.

Richardson the year before. Leigh-Mallory responded that the RAF had its eye on a piece of land, some twelve miles west of Newcastle: a small field not far from Ouston. Runciman expressed regret that No. 607 Squadron would have to sever its connections with County Durham, and distaste at the prospect of removing the name from the squadron's title.[12]

An annual visit to Mount Stewart on the Whit weekend was initiated in 1936—another occasion on which the pilots' social background came in handy. When the squadron arrived at Newtonards, it lined up alongside a Junkers 52 that had transported fellow guests: German Ambassador Joachim von Ribbentrop, his wife, and their accompanying entourage. Needless to say, this event, like others held by Lord Londonderry, received adverse publicity in the press. The event was repeated in 1937, but, by that stage, it is doubtful whether Runciman's pilots much enjoyed the company of their German fellow guests.

The squadron was invited again in 1938, on at least three occasions— once by telegram, stating that any date would be favourable. Every invitation was met with a polite refusal by Runciman, in which he courteously pointed out that the squadron was heavily engaged in training duties. There was truth to this statement: various pilots' logbooks suggest that training was underway on the Catfoss ranges at this time.[13] It is also possible that, in the run-up to war, the CO wanted to avoid attracting any more negative publicity; there is, however, no hard evidence to suggest so.

On 16 April 1938, Blackadder piloted a cross-country flight to Aldergrove in Demon K5891, with LAC Clarke in the back seat. This was a formation flight, for Blackadder's Demon was accompanied by the similar aircraft of Dudley Craig.[14] The flight lasted longer than usual, because the pair did not return to Usworth, but instead flew on to Turnhouse, Edinburgh. Once there, LAC Clarke was replaced with a sergeant before Blackadder continued south to Usworth, where he carried out a local flight. Two days later, he flew as a passenger in Demon K5693 flown by Jim Bazin, and the pair went on a cross-country flight to Turnhouse once more, returning the following day.[15] Blackadder noted in his logbook that he had been unable to fly as a pilot since 23 April, due to a dislocation of the shoulder. He made no reference to how he got the injury, so it may have been rugby- rather than flight-related. This cost him a month's piloting time in the air, for which he was not judged until 21 May.

While recovering from his injury, Blackadder was still able to attend flights as a passenger. He accompanied Runciman in Demon K5686 on a cross-country flight to Catfoss and back. Ten days later, he flew in the back seat of Demon K5685, on an interception with Jim Vick; he followed this up with an afternoon flight in Demon K3800, acting as a target in simulated interceptions. Both flights were carried out at 6,000 feet.

No. 607 Squadron and Blackadder, fourth from the right, 1938.

Munich crisis at Usworth: Reddinton, Gale, Sample, Gore, and Blackadder (from left to right).

Once fully recovered, Blackadder was soon back to piloting again. His first return flight was a short R/T test, followed by three successive flights in collaboration with the local Anti-Aircraft (AA). He took a different airman up in the back seat on each of these flights, giving them each a turn at air experience. The rest of the month was taken up with fighter tactics, except for a brief flight in Avro K2364, which he took up for a five-minute circuit and landing.

July saw a steep increase in the AAF's training and workload. Many of Blackadder's logbook entries record cross-country flights that tended to have reconnaissance purposes, and took him to airfields such as Acklington. Also woven into his training was air-to-air gunnery, advanced deflection, and practising all angles of attack from varying quarters (such as stern and quarter attacks). The drogue was often used, and Blackadder recorded a 34 per cent hit on 17 July in Demon K4542. Emphasis on fighter combat, and areas such as quarter and beam attacks, prevailed, with some height experience thrown into the mix, and Blackadder recorded a 12,000-feet battle-climb. But despite their busy schedule, pilots were still able to let off steam through the art of formation flying.

Fighter attacks and interceptions were much in evidence during the training programme. Aircraft alternated between using front guns and rear guns, and exchanged rear-gunners in their back seats—although AC Cole seems to have been Blackadder's favourite. Many flights went to and from the Catfoss, Catterick, and Skipsea ranges. Most of them incorporated R/T tests, so that pilots got used to their radio equipment. As the end of July approached, interceptions escalated and were coordinated with other squadrons. Two such flights were recorded by Blackadder, against Nos 608 and 43 Squadrons. Air-to-air camera-gunning, advanced and with deflection, were also recorded at this time. Skipsea boasted ten-foot-square firing targets, and Blackadder recorded scoring 41 points out of a possible 70 on 24 July; he then managed a 30 per cent successful air-to-ground firing there. These July activities were building up to the forthcoming annual summer camp.

On 30 July 1938, Blackadder flew from Usworth to the Warmwell summer camp, Dorset, in Demon K5692. This was the same aircraft that he had flown to summer camp the previous year, but there were no accidents this time. The event itself was originally planned to take place at Acklington, only a short distance north of Usworth, but Runciman had intervened. He had argued to the RAF that summer camp was as much of an annual holiday for his men as it was a training programme, and that, as such, Acklington would not fit the bill. 'They need a change of scene', he wrote, and the result was Warmwell.[16]

Training at summer camp began slowly, but intensified in tandem with political tensions in Europe. On the first day, Blackadder made only

Blackadder, far right, with ground crew.

Shifting the heavy snow from around a Gladiator.

one ascent in the back seat of Demon K5694, a reconnaissance flight carried out by John Sample. The next few days consisted of short flights, all under thirty minutes, flown against the drogue and firing at ground targets. Routines in the air were variously punctuated with respirator-practice. Blackadder made two flights with Will Gore in Demon K4542 on 10 August, the first with Gore as pilot and the second in the reverse. These two flights were listed as 'air-to-ground–rear gun' so may have been Gore trying to make a point of his skills. The last day at Warmwell was described by Blackadder as a complete washout due to bad weather.

After the 1938 summer camp, the majority of the AAF's activities centred on fighter offensives, air-to-ground gunnery, and attacking the drogue. However, things were all about to change. Among other AAF squadrons, No. 607 was absorbed into the RAF as part of the national response to the Munich Agreement, signed on 30 September. The Demons lost their highly polished finish and colourful squadron insignia, and were given a drab camouflage coating. Oddly enough, Blackadder makes no comment on this situation in his logbook. Two days prior to the merger, he had ascended in a formation battle-climb; two days, later he was carrying out a dual night flight in an Avro Tutor, K3407, under the instruction of Willy Turner. Yet his logbook makes note of only two hours of night flying at this time.

Camouflaged Demons around the time of the Munich Agreement, 1938.

Under the shadow of the Munich Agreement, Blackadder conducted a combination of offensive as well as defensive patrols. Interceptions of both bomber and fighter attacks were the order of the day, as well as simulated bomber missions on local landmarks, such as Dunstan power station near Newcastle upon Tyne—the power station was among those local targets thought to be at high-risk in case of enemy attack. Aircraft of No. 607 Squadron were requested to fly over many installations and report on their visibility from the air. Blackadder also records that he made bomber attacks on Catterick, Sunderland and the city of Durham— all were thought of as potentially high-risk targets. Blackadder's bomber attacks were even coordinated with the Observer Corps, AA, and local defences; yet, there was no call for mobilisation, and on 11 October, the squadron was once again disembodied. For its pilots and airmen, it was back to a part-time role.

The subsequent drop in the squadron's number of flights is echoed in Blackadder's logbook. What flights he did carry out mostly reverted to routine night flying. Night flying training began once more with a dual-flight with flying instructor Willy Turner. A flight in Hart K6482 followed later the same day, as did a solo flight in a Demon. The month of October finished off with practices of No. 1 attacks and more air-firing at drogues.

As they entered December 1938, the squadron took on board changes to national defence policy. Rumours circulated that the day of the Demon was over, and that it would be replaced with the Gloster Gladiator; No. 607 Squadron would be the first auxiliary squadron to fly this nimble little aircraft. The departure of a number of squadron members also had to be adjusted to—principally air-gunners, because their services were no longer required on single-seat aircraft. Their only choice was either to keep their trade and depart for squadrons in need of air-gunners—Coastal Command or Bomber Command—or to re-train as pilots; most of them departed. Joining them was the squadron CO, Leslie Runciman.

Apart from his work with the Runciman Shipping Line, Runciman had business interests in Imperial Airways and its merger with British Airways—to form the British Overseas Airways Corporation (BOAC)— in particular. Because he was living in London, he had little time to travel to Usworth every week; he therefore sought advice from Leigh-Mallory on his possible retirement, though he wished to actively keep in touch with the AAF, especially No. 607 Squadron. Leigh-Mallory came to the same conclusion that retirement would be the best course of action, which Runciman learnt with satisfaction. Runciman was accordingly appointed to the AAF General List on 1 January 1939, and replaced Lord Londonderry as the Honorary Commanding Officer of the squadron.[17]

Cockpit of a Gladiator at Abbotsinch.

When Runciman left No. 607 Squadron in late 1938, he presented thirty-six pairs of sterling-silver cufflinks, from Goldsmiths of London, as a parting gift to his pilots. One set was sent to the mother of Tim Carr-Ellison, who was killed on active service with No. 54 Squadron in January 1939. Runciman also had the squadron crest mounted and highlighted in enamel in the squadron's colours.

It was 1 December 1938 when No. 607 Squadron was officially informed that they would be re-equipped with the Gladiator. The first six Gladiators arrived at Usworth just prior to Christmas, so had little effect on Blackadder, who had already left for his holiday. The last three flights he made that year were on the Demon K5692, one for R/T tests, and two cross-country flights to Aldergrove and back. He would only face this new challenge upon his return.

Leslie Runciman's departure precipitated several promotions in 1939. Launcelot E. Smith replaced him as CO of No. 607 Squadron, Joe Kayll was promoted to Officer Commanding 'A' Flight, and John Sample Officer Commanding 'B' Flight. For Blackadder, the year began on 7 January, his first recorded flight in a Gladiator (a K8030). This lasted thirty-five minutes, long enough for him to acquaint himself with the new single-seat fighter. On the following day, he managed four flights in the Gladiator— two 'local', one as formation flying, and one as an R/T test.

According to the No. 607 Squadron ORB, army cooperation was arranged on the evening of 28 January, and flights were made in conjunction with the Tyneside AA defences. Although the airfield at Usworth was unserviceable and its aircraft not allowed to take off, some flights obviously took place earlier that day. Blackadder was recorded to have taken part in two formation flights, the first of these was in a Gladiator K8000. Individual aircraft letters were not recorded in his logbook during this period, but this aircraft became the first to bear the letter 'F', the aircraft normally flown by Blackadder.

There was a break in Blackadder's flying until 12 February. On this day, he flew three times in Gladiators, as part of a return to the fighter training programme: once in an 'E', and twice in an 'F'. All three flights incorporating battle climbs and fighter intercepts. This was also the first time he used a single letter to identify individual aircraft, though the beginning of this practice is officially dated back to April 1939—yet another in No. 607 Squadron's tally of firsts within the AAF's history. Although the squadron code letter and individual aircraft letter were visible on all No. 607 Squadron's aircraft, not all pilots made use of them, sticking instead to the aircraft number. Jim Bazin used individual aircraft letters from 19 March onwards, while Dudley Craig, a prolific writer and note-taker, did not use of the individual letter system until July. Some used either the aircraft letter or number until well into the war.

Blackadder retreated once again from flying—as was the prerogative of AAF part-timers—until 26 February. He then made a bombing raid on an unspecified target flying 'O', and in March concentrated on fighter attacks and tactics. He broke from routine on 13 March, when he flew as a passenger in Hart K6492, with Joe Kayll as pilot, the purpose of which he called 'dual aerobatics'. By the end of March, No. 607 Squadron was pronounced fully re-equipped with the Gladiator.

In April, Blackadder increased his flying, in particular in the Gladiator. There was some fighter work, and he carried out an airframe test on Gladiator 'N'. He flew in a bombing raid on 16 April, once again against an unspecified target, in Demon K5685 with Petty Officer (PO) John Humpherson in the rear seat. Humpherson was not an AAF pilot, but with the Station HQ at Usworth around this time; he is not mentioned in the ORB as part of the squadron until August of that year, when he was listed as at the annual summer camp. Blackadder followed this up with a solo flight up to 2,000 feet in a Tutor K3407. On 23 April, as though making up for lost time, he flew a total of six journeys: two tests in a Demon and four in Hart K6482. These were low-level cross-country flights to Turnhouse and back, Sqn Ldr Macdonald in the rear seat on the return leg.

On 23 April, Blackadder also had three flights in a Gladiator 'A'. His first flight consisted of straightforward aerobatics, listed as 'Loops in formation etc.'; he followed it up with a formation flight up to 3,000 feet.

The month of May was busier than usual, littered with fighter attacks and camera-gun exercises. Blackadder reverted to the Demon on 6 May on a short test flight, before departing on some cross-country flying. The first cross-country flight took him to Turnhouse.

On 13 May, Blackadder practised camera-gun exercises and acted as the target machine for other aircraft in Gladiator 'G'. Squadron drills were also flown and there was a break in routine as he flew Demon K5685. This was a short flight of forty-five minutes duration, giving members of the local press an air experience flight and the opportunity to see the men of No. 607 Squadron in their natural element, at altitude rather than on the ground. This was to give the press a 'taster' of military flying in the run up to the Empire Air Day to be held on 20 May at Usworth.

More camera-gun flights proceeded on 18 May, followed by more squadron formation and aerobatics practice. Given the date, it looks as though these exercises were part of practise for Empire Air Day, which was set to take place two days later. However, Blackadder took no part in this and fails to make mention of it; he records no flying at all between 18 and 27 May, and appears to have taken no flying part in any of the annual Air Days at Usworth while on the squadron.

On 27 May, Blackadder carried out three flights in Gladiator 'G'. All these flights were recorded as exercises and only lasted for an average of twenty minutes. Blackadder took another break from flying on this date, which may have been linked to business commitments. He did not return to flying until 18 June, on which he completed two flights in Gladiator 'D'; the first lasted twenty minutes, and the second over an hour. Both flights were recorded as camera-gun exercises. Like many other squadron pilots during this period, Blackadder did not stick to one aircraft; this later became common practice.

On the 24 June Blackadder undertook five flights, once again in a variety of aircraft: two in 'Q', two in 'H', and one in 'F'. Once again, their objective was the improvement of fighter tactics, with emphasis on the camera-gun, though Blackadder's role was reversed—from hunt*er* to hunt*ed*—when he flew 'F'. The rest of June saw him complete only four flights, and all of them in Gladiator 'B'.

July was spent in a similar vein; Blackadder practised using the camera-gun, beginning on 1 July, with a flight in 'B'. He followed this up with formation practice, a test flight in Gladiator 'T', a solo flight in a Tutor K6109, and another flight in Hart K6482 with PO Alan Glover in the rear seat (carrying out instrument flying).

Blackadder flew the Gladiator 'T' on 2 July, in conjunction with local defences, as part of what he describes as 'Observer Corps work'. Around one hundred members of the Observer Corps paid a visit to Usworth that month, to take part in lectures and various demonstrations. They were also encouraged to board flights in order to gain air experience, though this was not compulsorily. On the day of their visit, Blackadder took part in two cross-country flights to Thornaby and back in Gladiator 'T'.

Four days later, Blackadder returned to the Tutor in a short flight with Sgt Woods in the passenger seat, followed by formation flying the day after. He used a variety of Gladiators—for example, 'B' and 'D'—rather than a single aircraft in these exercises, but it was soon back to 'F', in which he completed a 30,000-feet battle-climb and formation flight the next day. He was back on fighter duty on 13 July, when he recorded a patrol, and took Gladiator 'L', the aircraft that was often flown by Dudley Craig, on a test—'L' had been fitted with a new radio, hence the air test. He also flew in Gladiators 'K' and 'Q', and finished off the day with a solo flight in the Tutor.

In a break with routine, Blackadder conducted Radio Direction Finding and co-ordination tests. On 23 July, he flew cross-country to Abbotsinch in 'D', and spent the night there before returning to the base. For the remainder of July, Blackadder flew mainly in formation and in 'F'; aerobatics featured prominently, as well as more fighter tactics, and these were practised on 30 July in operational exercises. The annual summer camp was fast approaching when Blackadder made three flights in Demons—two in a K5689 and one in a K5688—on 31 July. This was meant to provide airmen—namely Donaldson, Newley, and Smith—with more air experience, as was Blackadder's flight in the Tutor K3407 on 9 August. His logbook entry suggests that he may have had more than one passenger on the latter flight.

Blackadder next flew Gladiator 'F' on a camera-gun exercise. This logbook entry is dated 15 August, however, this must have been an error, because records show that No. 607 Squadron flew to Abbotsinch for their summer camp on the 12th. The next entry is for a formation flight in 'S', dated 1 August, followed by a test flight in Demon K5688, on 13 August. On 12 August, Blackadder turned up at Usworth with his suitcase in hand, ready for the cross-country flight to Abbotsinch for what would turn out to be the last summer camp of peacetime. He had no idea how long the training would last, nor when the war would break out. It was on this day of uncertainty that Blackadder began to put his thoughts, feelings, and the everyday life of No. 607 Squadron to paper.

2

The Diary

The diary of William Francis Blackadder was written in a service notebook. There is nothing elaborate about it: it has a plain brown paper cover, and on its front is a small representation of the No. 607 Squadron badge. Beneath this, in large, bold lettering, is the legend: 'Diary of 'A' Flight, 607 (Fighter Squadron), Auxiliary Air Force, Usworth. 12/8/39–4/6/40'. Francis Blackadder was of course a member of 'A' Flight and his diary describes the day to day running as seen from that perspective. At the time that he began the diary, he had no inkling of where the squadron would be based in the future, nor any reason to believe that his base would move from Usworth. He could have no idea of the various places that he would visit accompanied by his little book, nor that some of the men and friends whose names appear in it would be dead in less than a year.

Blackadder offers no hint as to why he began recording the events of the coming months. Possibly he thought that, with a world war on the immediate horizon, he had better to write things down for future reference. The idea of the diary being published almost certainly never entered his head. When I first read it, I was looking for specific information on his interpretation of events and how they may have affected others. At a later date, I re-read the diary as I was copying it down, and formed a different impression of it. It became a much more interesting document, far more meaningful than I had at first thought, and shed light on a squadron both at peace and at war. It develops through the Phoney War, and accompanies the first auxiliary squadron to mobilise to France on the long wait before the 'hell-hole' Battle of France.

There is no doubt that the diary began as an everyday *aide mémoire* to life on 'A' Flight only; popular belief at the time was that the war would be over by Christmas, after all. As the war unfolded, however, the diary

'A' Flight at Abbotsinch: Blackadder in front, third from the right.

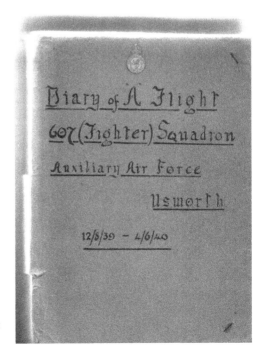

The brown paper service book that became Blackadder's diary.

began to cover more of the characters in No. 607 Squadron—and there were plenty of them. The diary also began to include members of 'B' Flight, ground crew, and non-flying officers of the squadron.

Nevertheless, this diary is in no way a gung-ho look at that battle, or at the RAF at war. It began as one man's recording of everyday life, not an RAF squadron, but on an auxiliary squadron. The diary developed into an important social history of No. 607 Squadron and its members in the Battle of France, and it is from this point of view that it becomes a highly significant first-hand account. Most of what is written within the diary's pages is missing from all other accounts of the battle which have thus far appeared.

The day Blackadder picked to begin his journal was 12 August 1939. This was the day that No. 607 Squadron left Usworth to take part in its last peacetime annual summer camp at Abbotsinch. Blackadder always refers to himself in the third person, and to his aircraft as 'F' (its individual code letter within the squadron). Blackadder invariably flew 'F', unless there was a specific reason not to, and individual code letters within No. 607 Squadron were jealously guarded like prize possessions. 'They, "F" and WFB landed heavily on the airfield,' writes Blackadder of their landing at Abbotsinch, luckily with no damage.

Upon the squadron's return to Usworth on 24 August, Blackadder notes that the airfield was busier than usual. The pilots' accommodation had changed somewhat, in that they were now billeted in bell tents and nights off in the Mess—their home from home—had been invaded by local soldiers in 'khaki'. The Army and the RAF had never got on well, and No. 607 Squadron's Mess had now been taken over by both bodies, as well as by local defence organisations. AAF pilots generally found this situation intolerable.

Blackadder's diary during this period leans towards a light-hearted tone, documenting various parties. On the night of 3 September, the day that war was declared, Blackadder, Gore and Dixon went on an enemy patrol—the first of the war, according to Blackadder. All they saw were various lights around Newcastle that could have been anything. The squadron next moved north to Acklington, because Usworth was being installed with two runways.

At this point, No. 607 Squadron had been promised that they would soon be dispatched to France. On the day of their return to Usworth, and no doubt after telling families that they would be crossing the Channel, the plans fell through. A couple of days later, however, they were ordered north to Drem, arriving there in the early afternoon of 16 October. The first thing that they heard was the sound of heavy gunfire in the Firth of Forth, which procured much excitement among the pilots—they were

No. 607 Squadron and Blackadder, far left of front row, 1939.

Tug of war at Abbotsinch: behind Blackadder (wearing the white shirt and white shorts) are Radcliffe, Welford, Glover, and Smith.

Tented billet at Abbotsinch: Pumphrey, Gore, Kayll, Glover, Sample, and Bazin (from right to left).

about to take part in the war, and as early as this. They were soon brought to readiness, and sent into the air at 3 p.m.: eleven Gladiators went on patrol—six over Drem and five over East Linton—with a total patrol time of around one hour. They patrolled the Firth of Forth in what Blackadder called the 'Battle of the Forth', and were fired at by HMS *Mohawk*, but that was it.

Around midnight, a signal was received, informing No. 607 Squadron to proceed to Acklington the following day. After taking off at 7 a.m. in the early morning frost, they arrived back there, only to find three Whitley bombers of No. 52 Squadron. These aircraft had been on a bombing mission over Germany and were led by the former No. 607 flying instructor, Willy Turner.

William Henry Nigel Turner, known to No. 607 Squadron as 'Willy', was a full-time RAF officer and ex-Cranwell cadet. He had spent time on overseas postings, mainly in Egypt, before qualifying as a flying instructor and joining No. 607. RAF officers were little thought of by members of the AAF, but Willy Turner was the exception to the rule. He appears on the No. 607 Squadron's official 1939 photograph, while he was still on No. 52 Squadron.

He was awarded the Distinguished Flying Cross (DFC) for his leadership of an attack on the seaplane base at Sylt on 19 March 1940; Blackadder

Gladiators at Acklington.

made a note of the award in his diary. On the night of 19 May, Willy Turner's aircraft was shot down near Ludwigshafen after an attack on the oil refineries near Hanover, and was made a PoW. He spent the rest of the war in German captivity, but pursued his RAF career as soon as it ended, and retired in 1957.

On 16 October, No. 607 Squadron was patrolling the Firth of Forth when a destroyer—later identified as HMS *Mohawk*—opened fire on Yellow Section. Luckily, none of the gunfire struck, and Will Gore even later recounted that he got a sense of lift every time that HMS *Mohawk* opened fire. Blackadder, on the other hand, remembered of this incident that 'the real war had begun'. The next day, the squadron was ordered back to Acklington, and Blackadder comments of the journey that the Border Country was looking its best in the dawning sun.

The 17 October procured excitement for No. 607 Squadron, when Blue Section attacked a Do 18. Although Blue Section failed to score a kill, it was emboldened by the news that the Do 18 had been forced to ditch. Another flying boat was attacked by Green Section—which was a second squadron 'first'—and Bobbie Pumphrey's aircraft got a bullet-hole in this encounter. Blackadder's next pursuit might also have given cause for elation, because it involved five 'Bandits' at 15,000 feet over Amble. Disappointingly, the 'Bandits' had gone by the time the squadron had gained enough height to engage them.

All was still recorded in a light-hearted manner until 29 October 1940, the day of No. 607 Squadron's first war-time casualty. Blackadder reported that he carried out some frontal attacks between 18 and 28 October, which would develop into a 'new form of amusement—dogfights'. The squadron still had limited experience of fighter tactics, but with mobilisation to France looking increasingly likely, the pressure to learn fast may have pushed some too far. Alan Glover, a popular member of 'A' Flight, was sent west of Acklington with Harry Radcliffe to practise dogfighting, and the two collided. Radcliffe made it back to Acklington, but Glover was killed in his Gladiator. Blackadder does not enter it into his logbook, and expresses no remorse or grief over the incident; merely, he logs into his diary that 'Alan Glover span into the ground north west of the aerodrome and was killed'. The whole squadron felt the loss of Alan Glover.

No. 607 Squadron's activity came into full swing as enemy aircraft began to crop up and paranoia rose to new levels. A Heinkel He 111 was reported—though never sighted—over Newcastle, while a wayward Hudson was spotted on patrol and mistaken for another enemy aircraft— the Hudson of course had RAF markings, but looked like a flying boat from a distance and according to Ops at Usworth, should have alerted them to their presence.

Rumours as to when No. 607 Squadron would be sent to France were still rife, and came to a head on 10 November, when an Armstrong Whitworth Ensign circled and landed at Acklington. Was this transporter intended for the movement of No. 607 Squadron or the neighbouring No. 111 Squadron? The pilot was questioned from all sides, and eventually conceded that it was here for No. 607. But why? A jerk of the thumb in a southerly direction was all the confirmation needed. The CO made frantic telephone calls to make certain of what everyone was hoping, and France it was. Spirits were high with anticipation, and the squadron celebrated on a last night out in Newcastle.

Now that war had materialised into a reality, many of the young men looked towards their future with less certainty: what would it now hold, and how best to tackle it? For many, marriage provided a sense of security, and in the next few months, pilots of No. 607 Squadron presented themselves to the altar, Milne Irving and Alan Glover among them. The newly married pilots were to join the ranks of the 'older hands', the pilots already married. Among these were Jim Vick, Launcelot Smith, and the squadron doctor David Smith, or 'Doc Dave'. All newly married squadron officers received a silver cigarette- box with the signatures of current pilots decorating the sides of the box; the squadron badge was engraved on the lid.

Weather caused many delays in No. 607 Squadron's departure. The Ensign carrying the ground crew had to land at Heston, rather than at Croydon, and left them to continue across London by bus. Once at Hendon, they met up with No. 615 Squadron, who had already been delayed. Eagerness almost got the better of them when they deliberated crossing the Channel in spite of bad weather forecasts, but sense prevailed. The two squadrons were put up in the Aerodrome Hotel at Croydon, and passed the time going to the Windmill Theatre and drinking in the hotel bar.

The flight across the Channel nonetheless happened, in dubious weather conditions and with Ensigns acting as guides. It took one-and-a-half hours to fly from Croydon to Lille, and Will Gore's 'Z' aircraft only just had enough engine power for the journey. The Merville airfield was a depressing sight; it was sodden, unfinished, and many of the machines were bogged down in mud. The officers were billeted in the town, while the ground crew were bedded down in the barn of a local farm. The boggy weather conditions of this low-lying airfield turned into an immobilising nuisance in the winter months, when the snow set in; the squadron would encounter the same problem later in Vitry.

Aircraft and machinery were buried in the snow, and the severe frost made ferrying men to and from Vitry a laborious task. Billeted out in the open, the aircraft were exposed to the elements and demanded more maintenance; occasionally, a makeshift protective tent was erected when ground crew were working on the engines. The early morning starts often proved tricky, because some engines would completely freeze overnight. Blackadder's plane, old 'F', was once damaged when one of the ground crew set off a light fire in the cockpit; there was little to repair, however, and 'F' was soon ready for operation again. Flying activities were regularly cancelled, not only because of the incessant rain, but also because of unappreciated visits made to the squadron by VIPs. Among the VIPs to visit and inspect the squadrons was His Majesty King George VI, on which occasion CO Launce Smith and John Sample represented No. 607 Squadron.

Pilots spent their duty time in the comfort of wooden huts, sleeping on camp beds, the idea being that this would keep them bright and ready for dawn patrols. The officers' actual accommodation was reasonably good, most of it in large houses and, if you were lucky, hotels. Some of these hotels were reputed to be the lap of luxury, particularly in Abbeville; others lacked basic amenities, such as hot water, or even running water in the winter, and officers often had to travel several miles to get a bath. For the lower ranks who were billeted in barns, living conditions were much worse—this was a different scene altogether from what they had been used to back home. Still, meals and nights out gave all of the squadron a welcome break from daily drudgery; many attached French menus to their descriptions of outings. The proximity of Calais was taken advantage of; some trooped off for coffee

Will Gore, front right, with ground crew.

Vitry with Gladiators.

and a look around the town, and even bought books of 'doubtful' taste there. Every week, the squadron gave two officers a weekend off, which they eagerly looked forward to; Blackadder and Dudley Craig once spent theirs in Paris, where they 'came up against the Duke and Duchess of Windsor'.

Rumours spread that the squadron was to move to Vitry—which had a larger airfield than Merville, normally used as an advanced landing ground for Blenheims—but facilities were not yet in place. The British National Defence Companies (NDC)—responsible for the erection of the new huts—were manned mainly by men from Liverpool and Ireland, and Blackadder's diary indicates that they often appeared too intoxicated to get anything done.[1] However, it was decided to move the squadron to Vitry anyway, and make do with what was there.

No. 607 Squadron moved to Vitry was made in December. The Royal Engineers were called in and had the huts up in days. More importantly, the Vitry airfield was more elevated than Merville's, and therefore less affected by rain and mud. Once again, officers were accommodated in a local hotel, while the 'troops' were billeted in a local farm. The downside for the officers was that there were no baths to be found in the area, except for in a hotel in Douai—some five miles away—at a cost of six francs.

While posted to Vitry, No. 607 Squadron also flew from St Inglevert. Here, there was a far better petrol pump, which gave the squadron a quicker turn-around. Winter in Vitry was, however, as bleak as in Merville. Aircraft billeted in the open air were regularly reluctant to start, if they did at all, so it was from St Inglevert that the squadron flew its patrols over the 'Blighty ships' ferrying troops to and from England. While at St Inglevert, pilots were billeted in the Hôtel des Bains in Wissant: it had a good pub attached to it, and rooms with running water (cold only). The lower orders were once more put up in a farm. Flt Sgt 'B', Barret-Atkinson, was nevertheless able to find a decent room in the same village, for the reasonable sum of five francs a night.

Pilots of the French Armée de l'Air were billeted in the same village: friendships were struck up, and visits to the French aircraft were made. New pilots arrived on No. 607 Squadron: Stewart, 'Chatty' Bowen (also known as 'Popeye'), and Gravstad were three of the new boys. Blackadder incorrectly states that the last two were Canadian; it was in fact Stewart who was the Canadian. New-boy Gravstad blotted his copy-book on a night out in Lille, and for reasons known only to him, made no effort to return to base; the CO subsequently confined him to camp, pending his pleasure. Gravstad did not remain on the squadron for very long; he was taken to hospital, and later released from RAF service on medical grounds.

Blackadder also draws attention to the life of what turned out to be the squadron 'Pig'—Gladiator K6137.AF-Z. This was 'Z', the regular aircraft

First officer billet in France.

Line up in France: Dixon, Gore, Thompson, Pumphrey, Parrot, Blackadder, and Smith (from left to right).

Another officer billet at the Hotel des Bains, Wissant; Blackadder sits to the left.

'Chatty' Bowen at Wissant.

flown by Will Gore, who had reported trouble with it from its days at Acklington. It so lacked power that Gore would dance around and shout at it; the carburettor was thought to be at fault, and a new one was sent from England and fitted on 18 December. However, 'Z' remained 'Cold and motionless' when an attempt was made to bring it to life. It eventually started up, but the trouble persisted, and finally came to its demise at St Inglevert on 7 February 1940, in the hands of Dudley Craig. The engine cut out at take-off, and a heavy forced landing was made, in which both the undercarriage and main longeron were damaged—'Z' was finally written off.

At St Inglevert, the frozen ground regularly resulted in tailwheel breakage, and this became a major issue. The tailwheel of Blackadder's own 'F' broke when it was being pushed into a hangar, and only four out of ten aircraft were serviceable. Red and Yellow Section were caught out in a mist when returning from a patrol over the Channel. Gore almost hit Kayll head-on, and Blackadder and Harry Radcliffe had a close encounter with each other, in which Radcliffe lost a tailwheel and Blackadder a mainwheel. Harry Radcliffe was known as the boy with long hair, and Blackadder recalls it standing on end after this close shave. Radcliffe seemed to have a talent for getting lost on cross-country flights, and did so on at least three occasions in France alone. After one such flight, Blackadder and Forster observed the CO remarking: 'Look at Harry—he's got his best bullshit face on'.

Harry Peter Joseph Radcliffe was perhaps the archetypical AAF pilot. He was born in 1914 in Malton (North Yorkshire), the third son of Everard Joseph, 5th Baronet Radcliffe, and local Justice of the Peace. Everard had

Blackadder and 'F' in the snow.

been a Captain in the Yorkshire Hussars Yeomanry, and was attached to the Intelligence Corps in the First World War, after which he became a stockbroker in Newcastle upon Tyne. Harry is thought to have been a graduate of Oxford—like his father—and later to have joined Everard on the Stock Exchange. He was gazetted as a pilot on No. 607 Squadron on 11 July 1938. Prior to this, he had made at least seven flights, all with Flt Lt Willy Turner, which began on 9 April 1938. He first flew a Hawker Hart K6482 on 29 October, and carried out his first night flight on 3 December 1938. The 'long-haired boy' was known for his light-hearted behaviour.

When Christmas arrived, the end of the war was nowhere in sight. When Dr David Smith, 'Doc Dave', returned from leave, he inspected the billets of the 'troops' and declared them unsanitary. New billets were hastily found in the Hôtel des Bains at Wissant, for five francs a day. Because it became transparent that the squadron would not be returning home, Christmas took on an increased significance for the men's morale. On Christmas Day, the pilots departed for the Wissant beach, where they played five-a-side football; that night, the squadron held a party with games, a hearty meal, and a song specially composed for the occasion by two of the ground crew, Story and Wright.

Although Blackadder flew on two patrols, the only event worthy of excitement was the sighting of a mine, which Green Section was ordered to patrol over until a ship arrived. A recurring grievance in Blackadder's diary is that No. 615 Squadron seemed busier than No. 607. This referred in particular to a No. 615's attack on a He 111, which Blackadder witnessed on a return from St Inglevert.

Under Secretary of State for Air, Captain Harry Balfour, once visited No. 607 Squadron accompanied by the AOC, AVM Blount and AVM Douglas. While carrying out an inspection of the squadron aircraft, Blount managed to push his finger through 'F's fabric; but on the bright side, he also gave the squadron confirmation that they would soon receive Hurricanes. The good news was followed by bad—as the winter weather closed in, water pumps, and even Blackadder's hair oil, froze. It was probably around this time that Jim Bazin took a painter's blowlamp to the engine of his Gladiator; the ground crew retired to a much safer distance.[2] A new pair of goggles was also demonstrated to No. 607 Squadron by Wing Commander (Wg Cdr) Livingston, and Blackadder observed that their field of vision was superior to those already in use—they did cost £4.

Heated discussions often took place at meal times. One tea-time disagreement concerned the state of the war in the air. Bobbie Pumphrey made his views known in citing the 'Complete disorganisation at Drem' (in reference to the attacks of 16 October) in his diary, a view shared by the Group Captain, who thought they 'Ran about like headless chickens'.

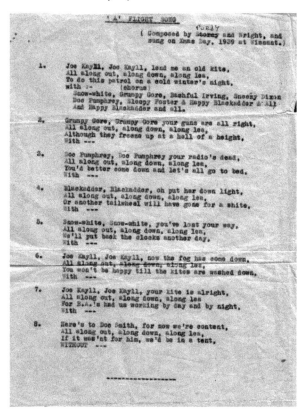

'A' Flight song composed for Christmas 1939.

The watch office, Vitry: Parrott, Thompson, Dixon, Pumphrey, Blackadder, Gore, and Smith standing by the door (from left to right).

Their own Wing Commander overheard this observation, and was himself 'Without noticeable pleasure'.

The Air Ministry Weekly Intelligence Summary (AMWIS) was read with great relish, on account of it containing an account of the demise of a German Do 18 on 17 October. The Do 18 pilot apparently commented, 'To be shot down by a bloody biplane piloted by a bloody barrister is more than I can bloody well bear'. Dudley Craig was the 'bloody barrister' mentioned—no doubt it gave great amusement to his fellow pilots. The implication alone that Germans knew about the AAF and its 'part-timers' was gratifying. However, the credibility of this article is questionable, and it is likely that it was in fact little more than a piece of pilot propaganda.[3]

As the snow began to melt and the thaw set in, there was a general feeling that the squadron might take to the air in earnest. However, low cloud and bad visibility kept aircraft on the ground, and even a visit from Churchill did not brighten the day. According to Blackadder, Churchill stayed for all of ten minutes: 'We were all ready for him but he had, "no desire to see us".'

On 13 January, Blackadder was leading Pumphrey and Radcliffe in section when he spotted a wisp of cloud forming high above. He set off in pursuit, and the wisp was joined by two smaller ones before the former dived headlong towards the earth. This turned out to be a Do 215, and eventually came to earth near Calais Mark airfield. The CO immediately got onto the telephone to his French counterpart for permission to view the

John Sample in full flying gear.

intruder at first-hand. A number of pilots were crammed into a van and set off to find the fallen foe. The smallness of the aircraft came as a surprise: it lay wheels up, and had no armament, though its cameras were impressive. From the pilots' point of view, it had first class instrumentation, with three compasses alone.[4]

Two days later, Blackadder witnessed the same scene near St Omer. On this occasion, though the high-altitude intruder made good his escape over the Belgian Frontier. Flying at an altitude of 17,000 feet, Blackadder could not make out any type of aircraft, friend or foe. Blackadder was leading Pumphrey and new addition Flt Lt George Fidler, an Armaments Officer from Group, who was attached to the squadron for fighter experience and flew his first Gladiator flight on 9 January 1940. On this—his third—patrol, he flew Gladiator K8030, 'B'. '"A" line patrol climbed to 17,000 feet in attempt to intercept "doubtful" aircraft,' wrote Fidler.[5] Getting around was still causing problems on the French roads, as became evident on 16 January, when the trusty Hillman van failed to climb the hill outside Hervelinghen, and reversed back to the bottom. This resulted in a walk of 1½ miles back to the airfield, and the section missing their first patrol of the day.

Though rarely mentioned in Blackadder's diary, Flt Lt George Morley Fidler—known as 'Morley'—played a bigger part in the history of No. 607 Squadron than he was given credit for. He was originally a regular RAF officer, who had joined the RAF in 1934 and spent most of his time posted overseas as a bomber pilot. In December 1939, Fidler was sent to Seclin as an Armaments Officer with No. 60 Wing. Most of his flights were carried out in the Tiger Moth and centred on his Armaments Officer duties. He appears to have gone home on Christmas Eve, and was attached to No. 607 Squadron on his return to France in early January. He enters into his logbook as follows: 'Attached to No 607 (F) Squadron for operational flying experience'. His first Gladiator flight took place on 9 January at Vitry and lasted twenty minutes; this was an 'air experience on type', and there is no record of the aircraft code or number.

Flt Lt Fidler's next flights were patrols, the first of which took place on 11 January in Gladiator 'Z'. He made a further six patrols before beginning a new logbook, mostly in Gladiator 'M'; his last logbook ends in March of 1940, by which time he had a grand total of 10.05 hours in the Gladiator. A further feather to his cap was that Fidler would be the first on the squadron to gain air experience in the Hurricane, on 3 March. He recorded no aircraft code letter or number, and the Hurricane was probably attached to 14 Group; the flight lasted thirty minutes, left from Seclin, and was recorded as a 'Type experience'.

On 23 March, he flew again in a Hurricane, on this occasion 'O'. This was a forty-five-minute flight from Seclin to Merville and back, seemingly

German Do 17 shot down at Calais.

An experimental Do 215 which was initially mistaken for a Do 17.

Bobby Pumphrey.

George Morley Fidler.

in connection with his post as an Armaments Officer, because it was listed as 'Air to ground (application)'. His last logbook states that he had a total of 1.55 hours flying experience on Hurricanes, and Blackadder recounts that Fidler had under 3 hours on Hurricanes when he took command of No. 607 Squadron. He must have gained little more Hurricane experience, if any, after 23 March. Most of his flights in March were related to his work as Armaments Officer, and these were generally carried out in the Tiger Moth. The rest of his logbook was lost in the retreat from France.

Until then, new pilots kept joining No. 607 Squadron, and not all of them were Auxiliaries. Peter Parrott, who had already converted to the Hurricane while at the Fighter Pool at St Athan in late December, joined towards the end of January. Upon arriving in France, his training took him a step backwards because he had to come to grips with the Gladiator. He piloted his first solo flight in a Gladiator on 3 February 1940 in 'K', which lasted forty minutes. The following day, he took part in thirty minutes of formation flying, again in 'K'. Parrott flew on 'A' Flight under the leadership of Joe Kayll, and later on under Blackadder.

In early 1940, heavy frost once more grounded the squadron, so much so that only two Gladiators could be brought to life. From 20 January onwards, snow began again to play havoc at Vitry, and the tailwheel situation was the sticking point. Blackadder taxied 'F' out, only to get stuck in the middle of the airfield, where 'F' had to be towed back by horses. Snow put an end to most flying activities, which gave rise to a general feeling of malaise in the squadron. Slight illnesses and further depression became rife as enforced inactivity set in. The beginning of February brought the long awaited thaw, but with it came flooding, which severely affected transport on the ground. The good news was that runways could be cleared and made operational, and restless pilots were able to relieve their need for the freedom of the skies with a session of low flying. Blackadder took old 'F', and indulged in some practice firing into the sea. Mines of every nationality were washed ashore in the vicinity of Wissant, and turned into the subjects of many a photograph. One dinner was interrupted when the explosion of a mine on the beach shattered and sprayed glass everywhere.

It was also during this period that the squadron was given a new address: they became the 61 Fighter Wing within 14 Group, 'a most pompous address with the formation of a new group,' according to Blackadder. No. 607 Squadron had been elevated to a higher rank within Fighter Command; maybe not earth-shattering news, but Blackadder felt it gave the squadron new credibility. He wrote with a flourish that they were 'no longer a mere Servicing Unit', in direct reference to a brief stay at Hendon where they had been dubbed the '61 Fighter Wing Serving Unit'—this had not sat well with the AAF squadron's sense of individuality.

The new Magister shortly after it was damaged in a heavy landing by John Sample.

The question of moving base frequently came up for debate in the run-up to receiving Hurricanes in March 1940. Would the squadron have to relocate to another base? If they were not going to be re-equipped with Hurricanes after all, what point was there? Rouen was high on the list, as was Le Touquet, but the latter was soon dismissed because No. 85 Squadron was deeply entrenched there. Another topic of debate was the return to England, but this too was soon dismissed. There was only one certainty—that the Hurricanes would never come, and that pilots would be waiting a long time before going up.

Blackadder received leave from 8 to 19 February. The trip home was a long drawn-out affair, as Blackadder described it, 'Due to all the red tape and showing of tickets' to board his ship. Back in England, Blackadder soon returned to Usworth to reacquaint himself with old friends such as Dob Wardale, Jim Vick, and Leslie Runciman. Vick had left No. 607 Squadron in France to take command of No. 609, but an accident had prevented him from ever getting to his new post; still suffering from a limp, he had been sent to Ops at Tangmere. Runciman told Blackadder that he had been granted his wish to visit No. 607 Squadron in France, as part of his duties as Honorary Commander. Their mutual interest in shipping prompted Runciman to show Blackadder his new hobby, 'degaussing' shipping in detail. On his tour around Usworth, Blackadder had cause to note that it was no longer an auxiliary mess. No. 151 Squadron found it easy to 'down' Heinkels, because it had been re-equipped with the Spitfire. The powers that be, mused Blackadder, clearly did not look upon No. 607 Squadron with the same sympathy—had No. 607 not 'downed' a Do 18, and was it not still waiting for the Hurricane?

It was on his return from leave that Blackadder learned of the demise of Gladiator 'Z'. As previously mentioned, its forced landing by Dudley Craig had been the last straw, and after lying in the field for a while, it was reduced, bit by bit, for the scrap heap. To raise their spirits, some of the officers set about sprucing up the Nissen flight hut; it was decorated, and most importantly, had a partition erected between the areas used by the officers and the men, to give each quarter its privacy.

Leslie Runciman visited on 24 February and a party was organised for him. The seating order was carefully arranged and Blackadder drew a diagram of it. On the 25th, it was arranged for Runciman to fly in Magister, probably an L5316, and Blackadder provided the navigation. However, a sudden flap brought the flight to a sudden end just after take-off; Runciman departed for Rheims by car the next day, and never got his flight over France.

To relieve tensions, a rugby match was organised with a local detachment of the Royal Artillery (RA), which the latter won. There was little fraternisation after the game, and no facilities for baths. However, this was put right a few days later when a party was held and ended with, what Blackadder described as, the usual plate and window breaking. Blackadder and CO Smith went over to Cambrai to pay a French squadron a visit; they met various French pilots, including one to be awarded a

Runciman's visit to France: ??, Dixon, Runciman, Pumphrey, Parrott, Smith, Blackadder, Kayll, and Thompson (from left to right).

medal for shooting down a Heinkel over Germany. They were then shown the squadron's fighter aircraft, Dewoitines, and compared them with their own Gladiators.

The weather gradually improved, enough to allow non-operational flying to begin again and daily activity to return to normal. The squadron practised with Lysanders, and performed exercises in the defence of road convoys. Typically, Battles or Blenheims played the part of road-bombing attackers, although the squadron was only able to practise on a Blenheim. This aircraft proved an annoyance to No. 607 pilots, because it persisted in circling around Arras long after it had been 'shot down'. The only good that Blackadder could perceive in this exercise was that they were flying again; otherwise, it was 'unsatisfactory'.

Meanwhile, the squadron faced a slight set back with Gladiator 'G', which was found to have a fracture in the longeron. The aircraft had just returned from Douai to have a new engine fitted, so the work of the service crews was cast over with scepticism: if one aircraft had an important flaw, were the rest safe? Will Gore was shocked at the news; he himself had flown the aircraft only a day or so before, and was thankful that he had not indulged in his usual aerobatics. The squadron was beginning to lose faith in its old Gladiators.

When No. 607 Squadron had first moved to France, the Gladiator was already thought of as a veteran fighter. This was due in principal to its biplane design, and in part to its inferior armament, and was why only two squadrons of Gladiators—both AAF units—had been sent to France in the

A line up of Gladiators at St Inglevert.

first place. The other squadron was soon equipped with the Hurricane, and on their visits to various French bases, Blackadder and his comrades were struck by the obsolescence of their biplanes. They inspected the Hurricane, its foe the Me 109, and fighters of the Armée de l'Air at close quarters, inside and out, and found their trusty Gladiators wanting.

Blackadder became Officer Commanding 'A' Flight on 13 March. The move was prompted by the posting of George White to Glisy, and caused Blackadder to ponder the squadron's loss of four of its original ensemble. They had always feared that there would be losses in France, but had expected them to be casualties, not promotions and postings.

One pilot was detailed to proceed to England and pick up an aircraft there. Feelings ran high once more, given that Hurricanes destined for No. 607 Squadron had recently been re-assigned to a Canadian Squadron. Was this to be a Hurricane? Would they be posted to Rouen after all? Or would No. 615 be re-equipped with the Hurricane first? A draw was quickly organised to select the man for the mission, and Bobbie Pumphrey drew the lucky ticket. However, it is safe to assume that he delivered them to Rouen and shortly returned to base empty-handed, in light of Blackadder's next diary entries.

A small group of men, including Jim Bazin, was ordered to Rouen to guard four newly arrived Hurricanes until their delivery to No. 607 Squadron was ordered. AOC Blount and Grp Capt. Fullard paid a visit to the station at Vitry, which heightened anticipation of the forthcoming Hurricanes. However, Grp Capt. Fullard merely lectured No. 607 Squadron on what was happening in the wider world and the perils of 'VD'; he made them feel 'rather like in the back of beyond,' reflected Blackadder. And still, no sign of any Hurricanes.

If No. 607 Squadron felt deflated after the anti-climax of Fullard's talk, it was definitely knocked flat on its back on 24 March. Four aircraft took off to carry out fighter attacks. Pumphrey acted as the target aircraft in 'G'; Will Gore in his new 'Z', Radcliffe in 'F', and Nigel Graeme in 'B' were to carry out the simulated attacks. For reasons unknown, Radcliffe and Graeme's aircraft came into collision, span down out of control, and crashed in a fiery pyre—both pilots were killed. Blackadder's logbook reads: '"F" crashed and burned out: Radcliffe killed'. Some publications state that the accident took place on 23 March, but this is impossible, since Blackadder was on a night flight in 'F' on that date. Many other pilots logged and wrote of Harry Radcliffe's death—he had been a well-liked if eccentric member of the squadron—and their entries confirm the date given by Blackadder. A funeral for both Radcliffe and Graeme was held on 26 March after they had lain in state at Vitry Mairie, and escorted by their fellow officers, they were taken to the British Cemetery at Douai

In France: ??, Stewart, Smith, Gore, Blackadder, Thompson, Pumphrey, ??, Radcliffe, Parrott, and Dixon (from left to right).

Peter Dixon (left) and Joe Kayll.

Kayll, Smith, Pumphrey, Blackadder, Thompson, Irving, and Gore (from right to left).

and buried there. This episode marked the end of Blackadder's time in Gladiator 'F' K8000.

The night of Radcliffe and Graeme's funeral, the lives of a further two pilots seemed in jeopardy. Dudley Craig and Will Whitty were caught out in the dark by an incoming fog, and temporarily went missing; however, both pilots survived—Whitty bailed out of his aircraft, and Craig managed to land in a ploughed field. Misfortune seemed to strike once more when Will Gore's engine seized at 25,000 feet in 'R', but he managed to land safely on the airfield. A new Magister arrived for training with the Hurricane. John Sample took it for a flight and, on returning, tipped it on its nose for braking too eagerly. According to Blackadder, 'Sample of all pilots—most of the pilots had done enough training on Magister, this was their second Magister, by this time'.

Four Hurricanes were still sitting at Rouen, and Dudley Craig was sent to relieve Jim Bazin of their guard on 20 March in Gladiator 'K'. On 5 April, Parrott—the only pilot on No. 607 Squadron besides Fidler with experience of the Hurricane—flew to Rouen in the Master N5755, and returned to Vitry in Gladiator 'N', with Joe Kayll as passenger. The next day, he, Jim Bazin, George Plinston, Cecil Young—originally of No. 615 Squadron and only temporarily with No. 607—and new pilot Trevor Jay—recently arrived from No. 87—were sent to Rouen in a Comma and

The remains of Blackadder's Gladiator 'F', in which Peter Racliffe lost his life.

W. H. R. Whitty.

The arrival of the new Magister.

tasked with flying the Hurricanes back to Vitry. Parrott flew the Hurricane P2574, which would later become Blackadder's 'F'.

For the time being, however, this was not for the benefit of No. 607 Squadron: orders from Group dictated that they were not to be touched until another four arrived. 'Were we allowed to fly them? Not on your life,' vents Blackadder in frustration, and his exasperation with patrolling 'In these bloody little biplanes' was shared by the rest of the squadron. None of the pilots were allowed even to touch the Hurricanes, which stood on their own on the airfield, and became known as the 'Sacred Four'.

On 6 April, Winston Churchill made his second visit to Vitry. According to Blackadder, this was primarily to visit 'his squadron', No. 615, but Blackadder informs us that Churchill 'Stopped no longer than he had on the first occasion'. No. 607 Squadron made preparations for a visit from their leader, but Churchill was apparently not disposed to see them. Admittedly, neither of the squadrons had their full complement at Vitry, because their aircraft had been detached to St Inglevert. By this stage, Blackadder had been promoted to the rank of Acting Flight Lieutenant, a paid and an honourable rank, as he described it.

There was jubilation on 11 April, when No. 607 Squadron received orders to move to Abbeville and take over residence from No. 26 (AC) Squadron, who in turn departed for Dieppe. Blackadder made the trip in 'Z', and Will Gore by car. The main reason for the move came some days later when, to the pilots' joy, ten Hurricanes circled and landed at the airfield—No. 607 was at last to become a Hurricane Squadron. While one section remained at Vitry for operational duties, the rest of the squadron were withdrawn from operations on 17 April to begin training on the Hurricane.

John Sample after a patrol.

Curtiss aircraft of French Air Force.

Probably the best French billet: Abbeville.

On 15 April came the moment that Blackadder had long awaited: his first flight in a Hurricane. This was a short 'taster' of some twenty minutes, and was carried out in Hurricane P2536, 'R'. The following day, he managed two short, local Hurricane flights in a P2571 ('G') and P2573 ('A'), and another formation and aerobatics flight in 'R'. Meanwhile, Blackadder still had some operational duties, and patrolled along the Le Crotoy–Le Touquet line in Gladiator 'Z'.

No. 607 Squadron's new surroundings at Abbeville suited officers and men alike. Nights were spent in the Mess discovering how rationed meat could taste when cooked properly, all washed down with local beer and wine. Before retiring to their bunk-beds, the squadron had plenty hot water for baths, a rare luxury since mobilisation. On the 17th, Blackadder got down to work with the new aircraft and managed four flights: two were formation practice in 'A' and 'G', and the other two fighter practice in the form of No. 1 attacks and gun-firing into the sea, in which Blackadder relished the recoil of his eight Browning guns. This flight was made even more memorable when the P2572 was given his personal initial, 'F', the second aircraft to do so. The old symbol was back, and Blackadder would spent most of this period flying Hurricane 'F', though on 18 April, Blackadder once more flew Gladiator 'Z' in the role of a target. Warming up on the Hurricanes proceeded swiftly, and most of the flying revolved around practising No. 1 attacks, formation flying, sea-firing, scrambles, and patrols between Poix, Amiens, and Péronne.

From 22 April onwards, No. 607 Squadron had more or less finished its Hurricane training programme. For relaxation, Blackadder and other pilots climbed into the Comma and the Hillman and took themselves off to Le Touquet. For reasons which Blackadder does not illuminate, Jim Bazin and Milne Irving got left behind when the others left for home, and had to spend the night in Le Touquet. They returned by taxi to Abbeville the following morning in a heated state. On 23 April, Blackadder led a section from Abbeville to Vitry, and carried out his first Hurricane patrol between Seclin and Douai: at 25,000 feet, they searched without success for a mystery Hun.

Blackadder's flights decreased over the next couple of days—he made only one flight a day from the 24th to the 26th of April. On 27th, he made two more flights: one in 'F', and a gun test at 28,500 feet in 'A'. His Hurricane conversion now over, Blackadder went on his second home leave.

Blackadder was still on leave in England when the German attack began in the early hours of 10 May. He returned to France in the company of Milne Irving; as they passed through London, they noticed that the blackout had generated an intense air about the place. Dover too was in a heightened state of alert. The pair knew then that the BEF had moved into Belgium, but did not know the location of No. 607 Squadron at that time. Irving hastily put together some rations of chocolate and wine before boarding the ship for Boulogne. Upon arriving at the French port, they were left in no doubt that the situation had intensified: German machines circled the town and bombed nearby airfields, and they heard five air-raid alarms in the short amount of time that they were in Boulogne. They set off by train for Arras, and after an overnight stay, they caught the first train to Vitry—to their relief, No. 607 Squadron was still in residence there.

Refuelling a Hurricane at Vitry.

It was from Will Gore that the pair learned of the squadrons exploits so far. Sample had vacated and landed his Hurricane heavily, spraining both ankles—he was knocked out of the battle already. Weatherill, a new pilot, had gone missing; he would turn up later, and Gore described his disappearance as 'money for jam'.

Blackadder's first taste of real combat came on 11 May. He had that morning led a patrol in Hurricane 'C', and reported seeing nothing west of Brussels. In the afternoon, he was leading Red Section (this time in 'H') and Jim Bazin Blue Section on a patrol into Belgium—in support of the BEF in the area of Soignies—when they spotted a lone He 111 over Aachen, and Blackadder shot it down. As the section moved on, it sighted and attacked a formation of bombers; the bombers put up a spirited defence with return fire, but even so, Blackadder shot down a Do 215, or possibly a Do 17. After this encounter, Blackadder saw a group of single-engine fighters and moved to join them, but quickly realised that they were in fact Me 109s. He evaded the fighters with a steep diving turn that took him to ground level. His Hurricane was running out of fuel and had an oil leak, and he was forced to land in a field near Hannut, Belgium.

Blackadder's story, at this point, can be best followed in a series of combat reports by the participating pilots of (his) Blue Section. They are listed below, beginning with Blackadder's:

Above left: Maurice Milne Irving in France.

Above right: John Sample.

I was leading 'A' Flight near Brussels. After a while a single aircraft was observed flying south-east some way off. We gave chase, found he was a Heinkel and after quite a battle, shot him down in flames (the bomber fell onto a house which had been evacuated).

Jim Bazin:

I attacked after one aircraft of Red section. Starboard engine stopped after attack. Blue 2 (Thompson) attacked later with quarter attack (after several aircraft attacked), Flames seen coming from port wing root. E/A crashed and burst into flames.

Thompson:

After one aircraft of Red section and Blue 1 attacked, I carried out two attacks from astern and quarter. E/A appeared to be in difficulties before I attacked. As I broke away, E/A was seen to be on fire and exploded on crashing.

Blackadder, again:

We circled round and I was just setting off for a patrol line when Peter Dixon, who had been flying on my right as No 2 called me up and talked of some more bandits. I did not receive the message but on looking round saw one machine setting off further east, so I followed. Soon I saw what he had seen, namely a score of black spots. We joined up and climbed up after them, and before we got near they had been joined by another large formation. Luckily two of the Heinkels dropped slightly behind, so Peter and I each took one. That was the last I saw of him. I had seen a formation of single-seaters approaching and imagining they were ours and having finished my ammunition, I pulled up towards them only to see they had rude black crosses so I hastily fled and eventually force-landed in a field due to lack of fuel.

Blackadder camouflaged his Hurricane as best he could with branches, went in search of fuel, and was soon off again. However, soon after taking off, he was pursued by Me 109s—with no ammunition, he was forced into making a low escape along the Meuse until he came within range of his base. Blackadder may have survived his first battle, but Will Gore was not so lucky; his Hurricane was set on fire, and he ended his days in a French hospital before he could be sent back to England.

The following day was a repetition of the first. Once again, Blackadder was flying 'C' on an offensive patrol when he was engaged by Me 109s

Peter Dixon.

and what he thought were He 112s, one of which he shot down. He was forced to make a landing in a convenient field near St Quentin, and was delayed from taking off when, on his search for more fuel, he was stopped by Frenchmen who were not convinced of his identity. A second flight followed—a patrol in 'G' over the area of Douai—without a sighting.

In the early hours of 13 May, Blackadder led an offensive patrol that incorporated a section from No. 615 Squadron. In the area southeast of Louvain, he spotted dive bombers attacking troops, which he identified as Henschel 123s. In the ensuing *mêlée*, Blackadder made three hits—setting one on fire and damaging two others—before he was set upon by a formation of what he thought were He 112s, and later turned out to be Me 109s. Outnumbered and outmanoeuvred, Blackadder beat a hasty retreat by diving down to ground-level, and passed through some telephone wires without mishap before he landed back at Vitry. Hurricane 'G' had taken several hits, and even the compass was shattered. Later in the day, he set out on patrol in 'F', but in contrast to his earlier patrol, saw nothing and considered it a 'quiet time'. Probably due to the pressure that he and the squadron came under, minor confusion creeps into his diary entries at this point. Blackadder noted that both CO Smith and Montie Thompson went missing on this day, when in fact Thompson died the following day, and CO Smith was posted missing on 15 May. The regularity of diary entries also lapses, as things began to move at a greater pace.

The 14 May appears to have been fairly quiet in comparison to the previous days. Blackadder made three flights on this day, one in 'C' and

Montie Thompson.

two in 'G'. The first patrol brought Blackadder into contact with a group of Me 109s; he attempted an attack, but found that his gun-sight was not working and the rheostat was turned off, so he once again had to beat a hasty retreat. Near Valenciennes in France, he came across some He 111s, and not being in a position to aim properly, fired his guns while swinging his aircraft from side in order to spray the bombers with bullets. This was also a day of reflection, because Montie Thompson, a long-term friend, was shot down and killed near Gembloux. New pilots Gerald Cuthbert and Arthur Le Breuilly were also killed in the same action.

From 10 May onwards, the diary no longer carries page numbers. Blackadder's handwriting becomes more ragged and spaced out, as though put down in a hurry. This may be accredited to the beginnings of fatigue, a likely explanation in light of the squadron's 'on-the-run' quotidian. Pilots taking off from one airfield had no idea where they would be landing, the stress of which was exhausting.

Blackadder's diary betrays more confusion on 15 May. He recounts a heavy landing at Douai in the evening, but this is at variance with his logbook, which shows that it was in fact the first flight of his day. Either way, Hurricane 'X' tipped onto its nose, records Blackadder, 'but lovely new rotol was a wreck'. It had recently been flown by Dudley Craig several times, and after this landing incident, there is no more mention of it. Although Blackadder made three further flights that day—two in 'G' and

Above left: G. I. Cuthbert.

Above right: Arthur Le Breuilly.

one in 'A'—he does not comment on what must have been one of the more important happenings of the time: CO Smith, another long-term friend, was posted missing after having last been seen near the Belgian town of Dinant. The squadron was now virtually leaderless, for John Sample's injuries meant that he could not fly and therefore could only command on the ground; yet none of this is discussed in the comments' section of Blackadder's logbook.

On 16 May, Blackadder did not fly at all, but there are no notes about a day off in his diary. He does have an entry in his logbook for a flight in 'F', but it is followed by a question mark. This seems to point to a forgotten flight or, more likely, a flight he thought he must have made. The squadron must have flown on this day, because Dudley Craig's logbook carries an entry for a frontier patrol. One thing to bear in mind is that the diary entries probably record events on the days on which they occurred, but the same cannot be said for the logbook, which was written days, if not weeks, later.

On 17 May, Blackadder escorted a Blenheim making a reconnaissance to the east of Brussels in 'F'. This he entered into the diary as 'The next filthy job': this as an apt reflection of fighter pilots' views on bomber escort flights. The aircraft escorted were predominantly Battles or Blenheims, and the targets were usually heavily defended by German forces as they advanced on strategic points, such as bridges. 'We were ordered to escort Blenheims on recce flights, but as they flew at naught feet we were of little help,' complained fellow pilot Will Whitty. Flying at bomber-level left the escorting Hurricanes vulnerable to ground defences, and many of them fell victim to flak. At higher altitudes, they became the prey of prowling fighters, in particular Me 109s or 110s. On completion of his escort duties, Blackadder patrolled over Hal, for which he recorded no sighting. A further reconnaissance was carried out after this, but he makes no comment of it.

Blackadder next moved on to an offensive patrol in the Landrecies, in the Le Cateau area. He met a group of He 111s and Do 17s, and claimed one Dornier. He made two further patrols in this area, and was fired on unsuccessfully by a Hurricane complete with British markings. The mystery Hurricane also pursued Gordon Stewart for a while, before it gave up on him as well. All of Blackadder's flights on this day were carried out in 'F'.

The 18 May was described in Blackadder's diary as 'der Tag', and in his logbook as the 'Battle of Vitry'. The day got off to a bad start when Blackadder and Gordon Stewart attacked a Do 17. Blackadder knocked out the rear gunner in one of his attacks, but not before the Do 17 caused damage to both Hurricanes. While Stewart continued to chase the Do 17, Blackadder was forced to look for a field near Valenciennes, where he made a wheels-up landing, sustaining only a minor bump on the head. Blackadder then made an attempt to disable his Hurricane, but not by fire (as was usual practice). With the help of some miners, he took out the eight guns and removed the compass and the sperry panel. He then borrowed a car from a local, crippled schoolmaster, and made his way through the crowds of refugees back to Vitry, over a hundred miles away. After taking care to remove everything, he omits to say whether he carried the guns back to Vitry in the car.

After his return to Vitry, Blackadder flew a security patrol over the base in 'F'. On his return, Blackadder was informed by Sqn Ldr Jackson that he would lead four squadrons on an offensive patrol escorting bombers to a target near Catreau, because of his superior knowledge of the local area. As it took off, the formation was besieged by Me 109s. Five aircraft were shot down, and Blackadder called the attack a 'slaughter'; luckily, he himself took off near the back of the formation, so was able to dodge the pandemonium. Blackadder was 'frightened' when, after a climb, he got down among the Me 109s; however, he did carry on, and escorted the bombers to their target without seeing anything else. Upon returning to the airfield, he 'broke down'. The aftermath of the attack, lack of sleep, constant moving from base to base, and loss of close friends finally sank in.

Blackadder went on a security patrol in 'F', but this turned out to be a quiet affair: and only one He 111 was seen at 27,000 feet, and this was too high to attack. What Blackadder described as the first Battle of Vitry then

Gordon Stewart, third from the left.

broke out in the early evening of the 18th with an attack by Me 110s and 109s; Blackadder was in 'B' on this occasion and got among the marauding fighters, but claimed no kill. Things went quiet when Blackadder patrolled the base in P3535, 'C'.

In the low light of the late evening, bombers were seen in the area of Arras, so the squadron took off to see what was going on. Under heavy AA fire, Blackadder closed in on the bombers he took to be Do 17s— which turned out to be Me 110s—and the two groups became engaged. While fighter chased fighter, German bombers struck at Vitry, dropping incendiary bombs across the airfield as well as along the Douai road. Blackadder was forced to make a landing at Douai as a safety precaution, and made the return flight to Vitry a little later than expected because 'C' was reluctant to start up again.

The airfield had been badly damaged, but worse still was the loss of aircraft, especially in 'B' Flight, and those that had been in the workshops had also been damaged. The decision was made to move No. 607 Squadron to Norrent-Fontes, which pleased Blackadder; he made the twenty-minute flight to Norrent-Fontes in 'C'. The move had come none too soon, for the Vitry airfield, village and surrounding area were heavily bombed again on the night of the 18th. It was beginning to get dark when Blackadder arrived at Norrent-Fontes, and ground crews did not arrive until around 3 a.m. Blackadder was fortunate, in that two officers of the Armée de l'Air helped him find a billet of sorts; other pilots slept where they could, and some, such as Will Whitty, spent the night in their aircraft.

The 19th was not a good day for No. 607 Squadron. George Fidler, who was given command of the squadron on 17 May, was shot down and killed in Hurricane 'C' in the area of Cambrai; Sgt Ralls witnessed his demise and shot down Fidler's attacker. Blackadder flew only once on the 19th, on offensive reconnaissance in Hurricane P3448, 'H', to the east of Brussels, for which both he and Jim Bazin had volunteered. Bazin received his baptism of fire courtesy of the British AA batteries, which fortunately missed their target, whereas Blackadder flew a mere 100 feet over a German mechanised column, and went unmolested in this 'not very pleasant job'. He arrived back at Norrent-Fontes an hour later; unbeknownst to him, this would be his last operational flight in the battle of France.

In the early afternoon of 20 May, No. 607 Squadron was ordered to vacate France as best they could. Most of the ground crew departed via Boulogne, and four Hurricanes were all that could be spared for the flight back to England. Blackadder was one of the five 'War-weary pilots' flown in a Douglas—the pilot was an unidentified Belgian—from Merville to Hendon; two of the other pilots were Jim Bazin and Dudley Craig.

Although not mentioned in either his diary or his logbook, Blackadder must have been sent home on leave between 20 and 29 May, during which period

James Michael Bazin after the war, Usworth.

he records no flights. From 29 May onwards, No. 607 Squadron reformed at Croydon to take delivery of new aircraft. On the 29th, Blackadder makes note of four flights on various new Hurricanes, in an attempt to find one he was comfortable with. The first was a P2874, which he flew locally for around fifteen minutes; the other two flights were of similar endurance and each recorded as a 'test'. His fourth flight was in a Hurricane from No. 17 Squadron—which he denominated 'YB-?'—to Kenley. His summarized his feelings about this last aircraft in one word: 'Impossible'.

On 30 May, he flew once in Hurricane P2874, recording a local flight from Croydon. Training began in earnest on 1 June to whip the squadron and its new pilots into shape. A number of Hurricanes were flown by Blackadder, but the one he used more than any other was the P2874. It was not, however, until 20 June that Blackadder added alongside this Hurricane's number the letter 'F'; this was the third aircraft to bear his letter.

While at Croydon, Blackadder lamented the passing of so many of the squadron's pilots, noting that only six of the original pilots remained. Some, like Dini and Stewart, had been posted away from the squadron and died within a short period—the former in an accident, the latter in action over Dunkirk. In the last of No. 607 Squadron's operations in France, Bobbie Pumphrey was shot down and posted missing; it was with some relief that Blackadder learned that Pumphrey was a PoW. However, Blackadder and the squadron were happy to learn that the new CO was to be none other than Jim Vick, and Will Gore also made a return to the squadron after hospitalisation.

On 4 June, Blackadder compiled a list of the decorations awarded to squadron pilots, rounding off with a DFC for John Sample and the DSO for himself. However, this same day was a momentous one for a different reason, for it saw No. 607 Squadron return to its traditional home. At 1.30 p.m., they took off from Croydon in sections of three; they flew over Oxford, Nottingham, and York, and came to a well-known landmark, the Penshaw Monument; soon after, they landed at Usworth. The airfield had grown in size since their absence, but for Blackadder, '607 had returned home'. Blackadder completed the diary with various lists of pilots, ground crew, and aircraft that had taken to the air, ending it with their mascot, 'Barney the dog'. This marked the end of Blackadder's diary—the King's Regulations dictated that servicemen should not keep personal accounts at this time, although the rule was not observed by others.

The last four pages of Blackadder's diary show a marked difference to the entries that precede them. The first noticeable thing about these pages it that they are covered from one side to the other in writing, and have no margins at all. They are also written in a different hand altogether from Blackadder's own, distinctive one, a variation most highlighted by the 'L'-like appearance of the 'Fs', which are practically written upside down. The words are so cramped that they are, at best, difficult to read, and tell stories relating to Peter Dixon. The first entry of these pages is dated 10 May 1940, the day that Francis Blackadder returned to France after spending some leave at home, and recount the experiences of Peter Dixon.

The opening lines detail how Dixon had been on patrol on the morning of 17 May over Brussels and was then granted leave, seemingly because he had had no second leave to date. He then woke Peter Parrott from his slumber—another pilot who had apparently not yet had his second leave—at around 3 a.m., and they departed in an ATA Ensign bound for England. Dixon and Parrott did return to England, and while there were posted to No. 145 Squadron—they later took part in the air battle over Dunkirk, where Dixon would be killed on 3 June 1940. The story then cuts back from 17 May to the 11th, describing in full the day on which Blackadder first claimed an enemy from a Hurricane, but from Peter Dixon's own perspective.

Peter Dixon's account of 11 May is, in part, similar to that told by Blackadder and previously recounted here. Dixon was also overwhelmed at the sight of the Me 109s, and he too was very low on ammunition and fuel. Making a swift departure from the fray, he lost sight of Blackadder, and was uncertain of which country he was flying over when he descended through cloud. He was hoping to identify Aachen Station when he was met with a hail of AA fire, and had to climb back up quickly. Again, he looked around for a likely landing place, and saw a shell-battered aerodrome that looked a reasonable possibility. On one side of the airfield was a road packed with fleeing refugees, so there was no point looking for fuel in that direction. Once Dixon had landed, a young Belgian officer came across to ask him what he was doing and what his nationality was; Dixon pointed to the Hurricane and told him he was English.

The Belgian officer then took Dixon to see his Colonel, who also questioned his nationality. After convincing the Colonel by showing him some English letters addressed to him, Dixon was sent off with four Belgian soldiers in search of fuel. Along the way, their car was forced into the ditch more than once because of low-flying bombers machine-gunning the roads. Eventually, petrol was found and transported back to the airfield, but on arrival, Dixon found that the airfield had come under attack. Standing in the open on the airfield, his Hurricane had made a good target, and was left in a smoking heap.

In an attempt to get to Brussels, Dixon began to travel with the refugees but quickly realised that he was getting nowhere. He swapped the stream of refugees for a car which he came across, driven by an impatient Belgian. Dixon called this part of the journey 'hair-raising', for the driver blasted away on the car's horn as he forced his way through the crowds. Dixon then transferred to a passing lorry of Belgian airmen—at least they were military men, and were probably more organised than the natives he had come across so far. For some reasons he does not give, he gave that mode of transport up as well.

Dixon had a talent for meeting the right people. He next came across a British Wing Commander, who just happened to be a liaison officer at the Belgian Army HQ in Brussels. After identifying himself to the Wing Commander's satisfaction, the pair made their way to Brussels without further mishap. The living quarters were a grand affair, situated in a large Château formerly owned by the Duc de Guise and on loan to the RAF. Dixon was shown to his room, which turned out to be a relative luxury compared to what he had been used to: the walls were covered in tapestries, which Dixon describes as 'fancy'.

After a good night's sleep, Dixon was encouraged by the Wing Commander of the Belgian HQ to publicly commend the RAF's achievements, in a bid to boost morale in the face of the German advance. All had to be delivered in French, which Dixon struggled with, but he did the best that he could. He was afterwards introduced to the British Ambassador—a man delivered oaths profusely—and taken back to Vitry by car.

The last four pages in Blackadder's diary were indeed in another's hand. When Dixon returned the following day, he told his story to Blackadder, who obviously persuaded Dixon to write it down. The last words in Blackadder's diary were those of Peter Dixon, signed at the bottom on the right; 'Peter, May 12th'.

George Dudley Craig.

3

Diary of William Francis Blackadder

Part One

12 August 1939–17 October 1939

(1) To No. 607 Squadron, The Glorious Twelfth had a special significance this year, for on that day we moved to Abbotsinch for the fortnight's annual training. Twelve machines flew as a Squadron via the east coast and Turnhouse; on arriving, machine 'F' and pilot W.F.B. distinguished themselves by having to land forcibly but without force and on the aerodrome. The next day, Sunday, was likewise memorable, for five members of the Flight climbed Ben Lomond, swam in the loch's cold waters and drank deep at the Buchanan Arms at Drymen. Thereafter the standard fell and customary camp practices were indulged in, each behaving more or less as was expected of him. But in the meantime, the international situation was becoming ever grimmer, so it was no surprise when the order to return to Usworth immediately was received on Wednesday, August 23rd; but the weather interfered and we could not get off. However the following day, Met Office stepped into the breach when the outlook remained dirty,

(2) and said that if we took off at 14.30 and travelled via Carlisle, we should arrive at Usworth in reasonable conditions. And Met were correct. At Usworth signs of flap were immediately to be seen: machine gun posts were manned by men in full anti-gas regalia, while we were immediately dispersed, 'B' Flight taking up position along the south fence of the aerodrome near the old ground target. 'A' Flight excelled and their aircraft made a line along the east boundary, starting from the sewage farm—truly a most unsavoury spot. Tents were pitched and in these we and our crews lived with a very occasional night off in the Mess, until some bright lad had the brilliant idea—caravans. So four caravans were purchased and

these quickly became more our home than the Mess, which had been made rather intolerable by a large influx of outsiders, chiefly khaki clothed.

(3)   Doctor David and 'that big black bugger' McCartney reaping a rare harvest, for one and all had to be inoculated, vaccinated and God knows what, and Usworth numbered over seven hundred souls: R.A.F., A.A.F., W.A.A.F., R.A.F.V.R, C.A.G., T.A., Regular Army, Civil Defence blokes and ordinary humans. David however soon tired and it required a messy axe-bechopped Vick foot to bring the gleam back to his eyes: this accident was a result of the decision to enlarge the aerodrome and construct runways, Vick and Kayll setting an example by felling trees. With the southern boundary fence removed, 'B' Flight retired with grace into the wood behind. Previous to this they had done well by inviting us to partake of non-alcoholic tomato juice and biscuits at their bivouac during their period on duty; 'A' Flight rose to the occasion, and seizing upon a coach and pair which happened to be passing the Mess about then advertising some film in Sunderland, they passed an amazed sentry and

(4)   drove in style across the aerodrome—and to each of 'B' Flight and 'A' Flight presented something suitable:

John Sample	—	a miniature golf club
Jim Bazin	—	twins in a cradle
Bobbie Pumphrey	—	wee man and woman
Dudley Craig	—	a bare bairn with a red wig
John Hawkes	—	railway porter
Nit Whitty	—	Easter egg chicken
Monty Thompson	—	goose
Harry Radcliffe	—	camel

while an extraordinary gift of eight corks was handed to John Sample from Flight by W.F.B.

Meanwhile diplomats of all countries were at work, with the result that at 11.00 a.m. on the third of September, a state of WAR existed between Britain and Germany. At 19.00 hours the French ultimatum to Germany expired. Germany had invaded Poland on the night of Aug 31/ Sept 1 and within three weeks Poland was mopped up. Russia striking a cowardly blow in the back at the critical moment:

(5)   and without firing one shot Russia acquired the lion's share of what had been Poland—so much for diplomacy and politicians. At Usworth mortals were still to be found, some of whom flew the skies while others

sat and thought and played games, some intelligent [and] others of the body. And on September 3rd at about 22.00, three very much agitated members of 'A' Flight, Red Section, Gore, Blackadder, and Dixon, were on the south patrol, looking for the enemy: this was the first patrol of the war. And for a long time it was to be an event of rarity. Flying was undertaken to help the gunners, the searchlights and the wireless folks, who were struggling hard in their efforts at DIF collaboration, and once to shoot down escaping Tyne barrage balloons. After Gore had failed to intercept, the intrepid Glover took off and quickly found his target, which was shot to hell at 6,000 ft but rose even higher until at 15,000 ft

(6)   it had had enough and started its course earthwards, until eventually disappearing into 10/10 cloud at 3,000 ft. But the whole countryside of North Riding was now rounded and many questions were raised.

Wars and Summons of wars—the second part of the well-known phrase acquired a new meaning for us at this time for each day on occasion each hour had its summons. Intelligence started the ball rolling with their takes of the mighty German Air Armada based in North West Germany, which most nights was definitely seen passing over Holland on its way here. Gradually we came to the conclusion that Intelligence did not receive Intelligence and their summons were discredited. Operations at Usworth carried on and from there [work] spread widely out / all and sundry, from the C in C Fighter Command at ACH crow were composing summons. Chief interest was over the type of new machine with which we were to be re equipped: Spitfires, Blenheims, Ansons, Defiants,

(7)   603 Gladiators, all fighters prominently. But one Gladiator had many hours flying to do yet.

October came and with it the report almost too good to be believed that 607 were to prepare to leave for France at once. New and exciting maps were handed out, [...] crews chosen, minimum equipment packed, and 48 hours leave granted, so that we feel sure that at last we are off. And we were mighty proud, for we understood 615 and us were to be the first RAF Squadrons to cross the drink. But it was not to be: we all arrived back from our leave keyed up to take off next am, but when the move eventually came—three days late on October 10th—it was to the north we went, to Acklington. However we consoled ourselves that this was for but a day or so and then we would be off. Hilas won. Another six days passed with nothing happening, and then a last a period of action began, for

(8)   on Monday October 16th at 12.30, we were ordered to move to Drem immediately. We shot across to the Wing Cos house, where we

had been billeted, pushed our clothing into our suitcases, raced across to out dispersal point, started up and were off the ground by 13.20. Half an hour later we were circling the old wartime base at Fenton Barns and both sections of 'A' Flight made worthy landings on a very rough surface. 602 Spitfires, Ansons and odd training machines were scattered around the aerodrome. We taxied over to the hangars and as we were refuelling, 'B' Flight arrived. Soon after, as we were taxing into our dispersal point, distant heavy firing could be heard and it looked as if the monumental raid on the Forth was fact. It was. At 14.45 the entire Squadron was called to readiness. Red Section (Kayll, Glover, Foster) took off, followed closely by Yellow (Gore, Blackadder, Dixon), Green and Blue. The real war had begun, and a destroyer going bats up the Forth opened fire on Yellow Section. All 607 were patrolling near the aerodrome at

(9)   10,000 ft and constantly closed section but of the enemy there was no sign: we got back to base, 602 had downed one and winged another, while 603 had also opened their account. Farquhar (CO 602) had chased III Heinkel 50 ft above the roof tops of Auld Reekie and this may have been the machine that came down in the sea off Musselburgh. We prepared for night flying but at 2.30 were released on the understanding that everything should be ticking over at 9 am next morning. Fighter Command Intelligence summary for period ending 8.00 October 17 reads 'Intercepted one He 111 10 miles East of North Berwick Fighters opened at 400 yds but no damage is known to have been inflicted aircraft is presumed to have carried reconnaissance. A raid of 9/12 aircraft attacked the Firth of forth from 14.15 and the engagement continued until 16.45. Bombs were dropped at the Forth Bridge and on Rosyth. HMS Southampton was hit but not seriously damaged. HME Mohawk escorting convoy (was it the ship who opened fire on Reds) suffered casualties from a near miss.

(10)   20 patrols were despatched by Turnhouse Sector and 11 intercepted the enemy. Two H1 111s were shot down by AA, one He 111 by 602 and one Do 215 by 603. Casualties among fighters nil. Enemy aircraft all fell into sea, four prisoners have been captured. Height from 4/10,000 ft and to have dived onto their targets to under 1,000 ft. No low level bombing carried out. When attacked enemy ac dived 50/100 ft above land and water and endeavoured to evade fire by turning. No skidding is reported. One He 111 throttled down to 120 MPH. Full use was made of Sun's rays and cloud in carrying out attacks'.

And extracts for the Drem official log:

13.59   6 Gladiators landed   (A Flight)
14.05   12 Gladiators landed   (B Flight)
14.35   4 Gladiators landed   (CO, Pumphrey, Humpherson, Irving)
14.45   All 607 ordered to readiness
15.00   Red Section ordered to standby
15.01   Red Section patrol Drem Angels 10 and shoot down any e/a sighted
15.04   Red Section taking off
15.07   Red Section reported off 607 to send up more aircraft as soon as possible
15.13   Remainder of 607 reported off

(11)

15.25   Reported 11 Gladiators in the air, 6 patrolling Drem, 5 East Linton; reported Red and Yellow refuelled fully. Blue and Green had 30 galls so approx 60 minutes cruising.
16.00   Green Section lands
16.10   Green Section returned to readiness
16.35   Yellow and Red now landed; no sign of Blue
16.39   Blue landed
17.20   Reported all 607 at readiness and they were ordered as follows, Red readiness
        Yellow, Blue, Green, available
17.35   All 607 ordered to readiness
19.01   Above order found to be an error and the state as at 17.20 reverted to

Late that evening the following telegram was received from the C.A.S. by Fighter Command and transmitted to us, 602 and 603. 'Please convey to the squadrons which took part in today's operations my congratulations on a very fine effort. They have fully justified the confidence we have always placed in them.' And so we were engaged in the first enemy action of the war over this country, and it was to Auxiliaries that the first German bomber fell.

(12)   About midnight the signal came through that 607 were to return to Acklington at Dawn; it was another cold but clear morning with a keen air and ground covered with white frost. Our machines were also hoary and required a lot of prompting before they were persuaded to run smoothly. However shortly after 7 am the first flight took off, followed in rapid succession by the others. Sun was about to make its first appearance for the day. And the sky was glorious. The Border Country too was looking its best, and far, far removed from the seat of war. We had no sooner landed

and refuelled than 609 were off to take our place at Drem. One Whitley arrived back with a heavy compliment of fitters and riggers while two more appeared from York: are under the command of Will Turner, who told us something of his trip over Germany with bombs.

Meanwhile yet another signal had come through warning the Squadron to be at 24 hours

(13)   readiness for service overseas. But with 609 off we cannot very well be removed from the Tyne Sector until they find another squadron to relieve us. However perhaps it is not so very important because things look like beginning to happen on this side. Zero hour today was again about 12.30, when 'B' Flight's Blue Section were ordered to stand by. 'A' Flight were supposed to be released until 15.00, but of course were immediately [made] available. Green Section (Bazin, Pumphrey, Thompson) took off, and Blue (Sample, Craig, Whitty) landed and history had been added to. For they had sighted a flying boat over 30 miles out to sea, which had immediately dropped down to within 20 ft of the water, it was only doing about 140 mph so they found an attack easy, but apparently, with no effect, though Sample swore he had his guns dead on it for at least 10 seconds, which should have meant a K.O. blow. Greens landed and even more excitement for they had encountered four seaplanes, again at a great distance out to sea, but flying at about

(14)   5,000 ft. Each pilot had delivered attacks, and Bobbie P had achieved the new [not] too enviable distinction of having the first two bullet holes through the fabric of his mainplane, but the enemy had continued on their course outwardly untouched. Meanwhile Red Section (CO, Gore, and W.F.B.) and Yellow (Kayll, Glover, Forster) itching to be off, and at last received the order [to] 'Patrol Amble angels 2', followed closely [by] 'five bandits East of Amble angels 15': by the time we reached this height, the enemy was presumed to be over Bellingham, so there was nothing for it but to pancake. We all remained at readiness until 18.30; but half an hour earlier the great news came through that the flying boat had been forced down on the sea and the crew taken prisoner. We had scarce time to digest this news before A.O.C. Saul arrived and showed becoming pleasure. A quiet evening and the next few days were reasonably quiet, apart from an occasional patrol, and no enemy. However they were filled with rumours regarding the flying boat until

(15)   it was finally established beyond all doubt that the prize was ours, moreover that it was so riddled with holes that the destroyer which had taken charge of it had no option but [to] give up hope of salvage and

send it to the bottom. A few days later a letter was received from H.A.C. Runciman in which he said: "my congratulations to all concerned and mingled with jealous rage at not having been there myself to lend a hand."

The Acklington official log for 17. X. 39 reads:

7.55	All 607 has landed
9.16	Green readiness, Blue available, 'A' released
11.00	Blue readiness, Green available, 'A' released
12.37	Blue ordered to stand by Ops Us
12.38	Us informed, Blue standing by
12.40	Blue ordered patrol Beer Angels 8
12.40	½ Blue have taken off
12.50	Green readiness, Red available
13.27	Green patrol Beer Angels 10, Red readiness
13.30	Green off
13.50	Blue landed
14.15	Blue readiness
14.25	Green landed
15.05	Red to investigate raid X.17

(16)

15.06	Yellow stand by: Red left ground
15.07	Yellow left ground
15.10	Green and Blue stand by
15.30	Green and Blue at readiness. Red landed
15.45	Yellow landed
15.50	Blue stand by
15.55	Blue on patrol

18th October–28th October

Quiet days, but considerable flying activity. Frontal attacks, and a new form of amusement—dog fights, accounted for most of the time although the weather also allowed for night flying and a section flew Tynewards most evenings. Kayll's 1,000 hours were now officially clocked up and in the cause of the first Acklington 'A' Flight party he tried aerobatics on a motor-car loaded with Vick, Gore and Dixon: an acute bend was not navigated with the following results: Gore did cartwheels along the road, first word on recovery satisfying and expressive—Fuck. Vick, Kayll and Dixon scratched their faces in a bramble bush: in addition Vick damaged his ribs so once more retired to his bed. Barney retired about the same time, so Doc had two casualties on

(17)   his list and as he remarked "I always had difficulty in distinguishing between them"—meaning exactly what? Gore and Blackadder also caused amusement on a patrol, when the following conversation was overheard:

W.E.G.	Can you see something?
W.F.B.	I can see nothing.
W.E.G.	Lead me to it.
W.F.B.	I can see nothing.
W.E.G.	Lead me to it.

After this there was silence, but both returned unscathed.

While at Acklington pilots worked their shifts:

Monday	8 am–3 pm	Red readiness Yellow available
	3 pm–10 pm	Red and Yellow released
	10 pm–8 am	Yellow readiness Red available
Tuesday	8 am–3 pm	Red and yellow released
	3 pm–10 pm	Red readiness Yellow available

and so on.

Our caravans had followed us up from Usworth and they were used by the readiness and available

(18)   sections during the day, and at first by the readiness section at night, but it was felt camp-beds in the C.Os room was a more satisfactory billet. At night the available section slept in the cardroom, until it was felt they could safely be in their own beds provided they had their flying kit by them, and a runner at the end of a telephone in the Mess.

On October 25th Red Section (Gore, W.F.B., Dixon) while on patrol did actually receive the command "No. 1 Attack—No. 1 Attack—Go" but our enemy hastily put down his undercarriage and fired two green lights at us twice in quick succession, so Gore decided to be safe it would be better to hold his fire. His suspicions were very much aroused and the section raced along until the aircraft was identified as a Lockheed Hudson with British markings—however it did look like a flying boat from the distance and apparently it had no right to be where it was, at least Ops Usworth did not know of it. In the evening the station threw a cocktail party to wives and others

(19)   but few of 'A' Flight were able to do it justice owing to the calls of duty.

Next day a Squadron of Hurricanes—No. 111 Sq—arrived from Northolt, their baggage and so on coming by Ensigns: they will share the operational work with us which should result in more leisure. After two months [of] complete idleness, they were keen to get to the North East where things were said to be happening—and sure enough within twenty-four hours of their coming, they had twice been on patrol.

Sunday, October 29th

Alan Glover span into the ground north west of the aerodrome and was killed.

Monday, October 30th–Friday, November 10th

Two sections of 111 were off about breakfast-time, as 15 Heinkels were rumoured over Newcastle, weather was lousy and they saw nothing. The excitement continued throughout the day, and various

(20)   patrols [were] carried out but nix doing. 'A' Flight finished the daylight period of the day by flying from their dispersal to the hangars with the CO en tte. The next days were quiet and the Squadron enjoyed greater periods of leave than it had since the declaration of war. What excitement there was came from efforts at low flying, but no untoward incident occurred. But on Friday November 10th there was excitement, for just as the twilight was turning to darkness a large 4-engine monoplane loomed up, circled the aerodrome and landed: this was the first indication anyone received of its coming. So speculation was rife as to who the chosen would be. Did it mean that 111 were on the move again or had 607 at last received their marching orders? A few words from

(21)   the pilot of the Ensign cleared the question. He had come to transport 607 there, pointing with his thumb to the south. The CO was quite taken aback and it needed considerable telephoning before he could

discover that this was so. Orders were given to prepare to leave for France at 8.30 tomorrow, Saturday, November 11th.

Wednesday, November 15th

Tomorrow came and with it dirty weather in the South: we requested permission to proceed as far as Catterick so that we could then make Croydon in one hop, but this was not granted: so we twiddled out thumbs, listened to a fatherly speech by A.O.C. Saul, who showed the expected paternal line when we interpreted his kind statement that we could push off for the evening too literally, and taxied our machines across from the dispersal point to bed them in the hangar. But it was only 16.30 and it wouldn't be dark for another hour, so back they had to go. However

(22)   they returned very shortly after his back had been turned and the Squadron proceeded to enjoy itself at the Station Hotel in Newcastle.

Sunday was an even filthier day with ne'er a chance of our taking off, so we again prepared for the morrow. First reports on Monday were not helpful, but towards midday the weather on our route was reported to be clearing, so we made ready. But a further interference, as a large hostile armada was reported and the entire Squadron was brought to readiness in addition to 111. After ¾ hour we were released and taxied back to the hangars: however no sooner had we gotten there, than the order to set out on our great adventure immediately came through. 'A' Flight C.O, Gore [and] Blackadder as Reds and Kayll, Irving, [and] Forster as Yellows escorted the first Ensign on a course which led us over Wylam, Catterick, York to Digby, where we refuelled and had a few words with James McComb and Jack Heather; another devious route

(23)   brought us to the outskirts of London [in pencil: balloon aircraft grave] where we said farewell to our Ensign which landed at Heston: later we learned this was a mistake and that both Ensigns and the other transport machine should have continued on with us to Croydon. So James Vick, George White and Graham (who had been posted to us from 602 to act as Operations Officer) along with our troops had to cross London by bus in a black-out, which did not please them. 615 had already been at Croydon several weeks and had been waiting since Saturday for favourable weather to take off, we were to go into the same aerodrome at Merville under 61 Fighter Wing Servicing Unit. We saw our machines to bed in the hangar, then most of us took a taxi into town, dined well and saw the show at the

Windmill. One or two stayed behind and went to the NAAF I hall to see the film version of "The 39 Steps".

Tuesday saw bad weather again hold us

(24)   up, though we very nearly managed to nip across between two cold fronts. However no one was really sorry for it would not have been a pleasant trip and we wanted a real night off in town. Eight of us, mostly 'A' Flight, went to the first house of the Palladium and saw the Crazy Gang in 'The Little Dog Laughed'—we went on to the Brasseur Universelle where we had arranged to meet Minnie Manton. He turned up looking younger than ever. A meal was held at Stories, then back to the Aerodrome Hotel at Croydon, where both Squadrons of Auxiliaries were putting up.

The fifteenth brought better luck and we got off just before midday: the weather was not too good but our Ensigns were reliable guides: the crossing across the water—said to be 88 miles—was uneventful, though Will Gore with his shady % [*sic*] engine was glad to see Le Tréport: One hour and a half and we reached the industrial area near Lille. The aerodrome at Merville was very sodden

(25)   and several machines stuck in the mud when taxying but there were no casualties. Our Mess is in the town, while we are all billeted out. Et voici la France. [In pencil:] W/Co Boret to meet us half way up with a/c.

Thursday, November 16th

A lot of organising to be done, after Wing Co Boret had spoken to us in the Operations Room, suitably situated in a farmhouse, [and] we set about various jobs. The rain fell incessantly and we received a further introduction to Flanders and after lunch a section from each Squadron set out by air to visit the French Squadrons of Curtiss Fighters at Auchy some twenty miles away. Kayll, Forster and Blackadder went from 607 but as the weather became worse they had to return by bus. They were very impressed with the American machine, which was perfectly finished and very roomy: same speed as our Hurricanes but mounting only 4 Browning guns, though latest models have six. Also saw a Potez 63a fighter bomber, which is attached to each Fighter Sq of the Arme de La Air [Armée de L'Air] and acts as a bomber

(26)   Station when the Squadron is operating far from its base. The French had dispersed the customary hospitalities and all were pleased.

Friday, November 17th

Gore, Blackadder and Forster brought back the 'A' Flight Gladiators from Auchy. Most of the day was passed in reconnaissance flights as we do not become operational until tomorrow. Just at lunch a tragedy occurred as Barney was run over and had to be shot: B-A, terribly cut up. In the course of the pm flying Harry Radcliffe disappeared and it was not until dusk had fallen that we learned he had lost himself and forcelanded happily fifteen KMs away: apparently he had previously landed at a French aerodrome and asked Oi Suis—le? This was near St Omer and they had directed him back, but unfortunately once again he took the wrong turning and dusk was falling when he decided to sit down in the first suitable field. At a local pub

(27)   where Vick, Kayll, Sample, Bazin, Blackadder and Irving are staying and where most of us fed on omelettes. Consternation was caused by the arrival of the gendarmes from Dunkirk who raised hell as drinks were being served after 9 pm. However after several tense moments all ended happily. The pub is run by a Frenchie, his mother, wife and four or more daughters aged 16 [or] less, who rush about the place like busy bees and talk far too much.

Saturday, November 18th

'A' Flight were supposed to be operating but our A.O.C. Air V—M Blount, OBE, MC, etc—had decided to come and inspect us, so a parade was held in the silo, where both Squadrons' troops are living. Just as we were [waiting] for [Blount's] arrival, an air-raid warning sounded, and throughout his inspection and tirade we listened for the enemy machine, but all we heard was the drone of our own Hurricanes. We went across to our own machines as soon as the parade was over

(28)   and by midday we could claim the honour of being the first Auxiliary Flight to be operational in France. Will Gore had meanwhile succeeded in flying Radcliffe's machine back, after a rather tricky take off. Blue Section of 'B' Flight went to an aerodrome near Calais to operate. Green was at available, while one section of 615 patrolled Lille–Merville at 18,000 ft for an hour and another 615 Flight operated from Le Touquet. As readiness Flight we were not called upon to fly and at 17.00 hours were released until 22.00 when we came on again. Sleeping in camp-beds in the hut near our machines; reason for this was to make sure we

were ticking over at dawn. Clocks put an hour back tonight. At Supper Radcliffe gave a brief résumé of his life in these words: 'I've fallen only a few times but I've played the fool like Hell!' Three machines from 615 under their C.O Harvey took off after 17.00, were overtaken by the dusk and had all to force-land, fortunately with no damage to the personnel. We had an uncomfortable night in the hut near our machines as the rain fell hard—the wind blew strong, so that finally at 5 am we all turned out and swung them into wind. A quiet day but in the evening a part of us went into Bethune and dined well at the Cafe du Vieix Beffrai [Café du Vieux Beffroi]: aperitif, soup, cheese omelette deliciously done, chicken and some very good cheese together with Champagne (24 francs a bottle) Pommard 1928, liqueur, coffee and [...] tip worked out at 50 francs or 5/6 a head! We sung our way home. [Written in pencil:] I cook few on gin.

Monday, November 20th

An uneventful morning as we spotted our first enemy machine—a Heinkel 111—Red Section (Gore, Forster, Dixon) actually saw it emerge from a cloud 100 ft above and some distance to the rear: on seeing it they immediately

(30)   sought refuge again in the clouds and they were unable to deliver an attack. However it did appear plumb over the aerodrome and seemed to take photographs. A further section despatched after it but without success. In the afternoon Radcliffe distinguished himself by making his second disappearance: on this occasion he turned up some 25 Kms South of Arras in a ploughed field when doing local flying. A Mess meeting was held in the evening.

Tuesday, November 21st

Joe Kayll flew Radcliffe's machine out of the ploughed field in the morning. 'A' Flight were released today and Vick, Kayll, Gore, Irving, Blackadder—Dixon went into Lille by lorry together with an unidentified member of 615. A fairly extensive survey of the town and its attractions was held, so that our next visit should have more definite entertainment. We dined at the Hotel Bellevue and visited the Cafe Jean, Miami, Olympia and Liliana, the rest being dancing dives.

Wednesday, November 22nd

'A' Flight at readiness. Thick air and ground

(31)   mist. Both stations were given a scramble in this, but were ordered to pancake when Ops appreciated the weather situation. Yellow did, but Gore was going bats out for Arras and it took Blackadder–Dixon a good 10 mins before they could round him off. They were unable to locate base but fortunately were given a bandit over Amiens at 22,000 ft to chase, also the correct course to steer. On the way considerable A.A. fire on the right and shortly afterwards a twin engined bomber crossed their path: it was not recognised as a friendly Blenheim until W.F.B. had fired a warning burst, though not at it. A very tricky job finding the base as there was still a thick haze, but Gore's navigation stood the test. A Blenheim continued to irritate us by flying round and round the aerodrome apparently taking photos but it fired the correct recognition signal so was presumed friendly. A section of Curtiss Hawks gave a fine exhibition of formation flying at low altitude after lunch.

(32)   Thursday, November 23rd

[Entered up the side of (34):] Make more of our landing: Vick in Ops landed almost went over.

Quiet days with no sign of the enemy: following routine now in force.

1st day—to immediate readiness
2nd day—30 minute readiness
3rd day—15 minute readiness
4th day—released and so back to 15 mins, this together with the long evenings—it is dark at 4.30 pm, allows us more time off than during any period since our return from Abbotsinch in August.

Lille has supplanted Bethune as a haunt for the evening and at the Metropole one can feed well, while there is dancing at the Miami below the Cafe Jean, Rio, Olympia and Lilianna and exhibitions almost everywhere. And for the gourmet there is the Maison Andre, a small family restaurant in a curious back street, La Rue de l' Arc: we were introduced to this place by the French Captain Boucher whose two Army motor crews frequently stand at our disposal. The terrain at Merville was incapable of standing up to the winter weather of Flanders and we were lucky to see only one machine go up on its nose, though others were frequently bogged. We had a North and West patrol, but the one most

(33)   favoured seemed to be Hazebrouck–Douai–Arras–Doulliers: when on this patrol at 20,000 ft you could see England, Belgium, Holland and perhaps Germany and Luxembourg!

Blackadder and Craig in unexpected week-end leave in Paris, a favour to be accorded to one officer of each Flight every week. They went off from Lille on Nov 24 and returned late on the 27th. The train journey lasted 3½ hours but a restaurant car was attached. In Paris they came up against the Duke and Duchess of Windsor, met the British Air Attaché G/Cpt Collyer and his wife and appeared in general to have had a good time.

[Added to side of page:] Men visit Bethune, Armentieres—Joe [and] Launce with ourselves behind to cross Belgian Border on way home from Lille.

On November 30th a dining-in night was held at the Mess to bid our adieu to Wing Co Boret who is going to group, and to welcome his successor Wing Co Eccles, a very quiet man. Boret made his classic reply: 'So what'.

Invitations to French messes began to flow in, and small parties of officers would go out and come back very drunken having fulfilled their duty and soon regretting it.

On Wednesday, December 6th, the Wing Co,

(34)   the two C.Os, John Sample and Tony Thornaby (615) together with a number of troops went over to Seclin (where 85 & 87 are stationed, outside Lille) and were inspected by H.M the King: Load Group in attendance. 'A' Flight were at readiness and did not get any amusement until just after they had been released, when Red Section (Gore, Blackadder, Dixon) were ordered to stand by—took off to patrol base: they climbed above the clouds, but no sign of the enemy. So after some good navigation by Gore returned and landed in the gloaming. Two days later more excitement in 'A' Flight when Johnson let off a very-light inside the cockpit of 'F' after accidently pulling the trigger: a hell of a lot of smoke and a fair sized fire, but luckily no one was injured and the damage to the machine was repaired by nightfall. All these days Gore and 'Z' were in opposition until eventually he took it up and practiced all the devilry his fruitful mind could evoke without any retort. Three machines also flew over to Douai and carried out experimental fighter

(35)   attacks on Lysander's. Slow progress was made at Vitry, where the Squadron are to hibernate as most of the British N.D.C. workmen who

were responsible for the erection of the huts etc were generally either drunk or else in prep for cracking a still. However eventually arrangements were made for the Squadron to move there, by Wednesday, December 13th. On the 11th Vick & Kayll returned from Paris with Captain Boucher having had an even busier time than the boldest had dared foretell. (More details of this. Russian girls 122 Rue de Provence.)

Good news yet sad. A signal came through posting Vick to 609 Squadron to take command from Ambler, who rumour has it is now a Wing Co and posted to Seclin. On Tuesday the 12th James took his farewell and disappeared from the champagne table into the night towards England.

Wednesday, December 13th

[Entered up the side of (35):] Description of Duty Controller at night: Describe Ops room wt set & table A at Arras & Lille. Mindful of sense ... this is with an arrow pointing to Duty Controller ...

[Entered up the side of (37):] Will Gore and W.F.B. interview Gendarme assisted at birth of a calf.

Not excellent weather for flying, but good enough to allow both Squadrons to fly across happily to Vitry with one exception. Gore and 'Z' were most unhappy and both were relieved

(36)   when they had solid earth below them again. The aerodrome was even larger than Merville and in much better condition: it lies on high ground so remains comparatively dry when there are floods elsewhere. As it is used as an advanced landing ground for a Blenheim bomber Squadron its defence is above par, with gun posts every few yards while piles of bombs of various sizes are stacked at odd spots here and there on the edge of the aerodrome. Our boundary is formed by the main Douai–Arras road, while to its North runs a railway to Lens, so it should not be difficult to locate. The huts (one for each Flight and one readiness hut) were not ready on our arrival but a party of R.E.s had been called in and they soon had the job done. The Liverpool–Irish N.D.C. fellows had the town of Vitry dead scared of them. Only a few days before three of them had kicked the brains out of the then Sergeant Major: they had been shot on the following day. But altogether we were not surprised at the somewhat frigid reception

(37)   accorded to us by the populace. First impressions were that the toilets for officers was not so good as our previous ones, while the troops frankly considered they were being treated like cattle as they were quartered in barns.

Fortunately time proved the healer, and the French farmer dealt kindly with them, when they realised these were not of the Liverpool–Irish sort. The officers Mess was the Hotel de D———, a fair sized building adjoining the station: it had a large dining room and a bar come sitting room of similar size and there are four small rooms on the first floor; the only point in which it lost comparison with the Merville Mess was that it lacked a bath, indeed there does not seem to be a single bath of any description in the whole town. So a journey into Douai—5 miles—was necessary and there you could bathe either at the public baths or in the Hotel de Grand for 6 francs including three small towels. But the greatest blessing of all was that there was no mud and one could keep reasonably

(38)   clean, and aeroplanes had no occasion to tip up.

Thursday, December 14th–Wednesday, December 20th

Cold weather with bitterly North East winds coincided with the change over, and our machines took more and more umbrage at being billeted in the open air. The dispute between Gore and 'Z' advanced one more stage when a new carburettor was ordered. Night life continued as before with Lille the chief attraction: Douai was near at hand but disappointing, the one big cafe, the Hotel de Paris, being expensive and crowded more especially with members of the British Army. The entrance to both it and the Hotel Grand cafe was restricted to officers. Lille on the other hand could be reached from Douai in ½ hour by express train and one hour by 'omnibus' ie a train which stops at every station and frequently more after that. Moreover is the matter of expense one more than saved the cost of the rail fare (9 francs return 2nd class) on the bill of fare.

December 16th Kayll & Forster by some

(39)   foul means were offered the use of a 7 seater Renault by the local garage proprietor provided they drove it them themselves. They asked for nothing better and that very evening they set out with Kayll at the wheel, and Irving, Blackadder, Pumphrey and Thompson as ballast, ostensibly for Douai. Two hours at the Hotel de Paris sufficed to convince them that Douai was a poor spot, so popular vote took them to the station and by 'omnibus' to Lille: while Irving, Forster [and] Thompson tittle-tattled at the Rio, Kayll, Blackadder and Pumphrey dined at the H—; on snails and oysters, sole, grilled kidneys, crepe suzette, Coupe Dame Blanche and cafe sarka covered all three, while the [befriended?] patron's recommendation of white wine was followed.

Also on the 16th, three new recruits to the Squadrons officers arrived: one to do operations (Stewart), one for 'A' Flight (Gravstad), and one for 'B' (Bowen), the latter two being Canadians, however

(40)   still no news either of Doctor David, personnel to have left Usworth on or about Dec 8th or of the new parties of either Squadron.

The weather was not good for flying but on our ½ hour day we were able to carry out a Sector reconnaissance of part of the Sector [between] Aras, Lens, Seclin, Douai, passing en route the Canadian War Memorial at Vimy. [Entered up the side:] Johnnie, Dudley, Nit at Calais: Moi then Watering from the sky.

Most cheering news came from our first big Naval victory making good the loss of the courageous *Rawalpindi*: the German pocket battleship *Graf Von Spee* was cornered by our cruisers *Exeter*, *Achilles* and *Ajax* off the South American coast, and after a fierce battle was forced to seek shelter in the coastal waters of Uruguay. It had been badly damaged. Our cruisers were joined by the French battleship *Dunkerque*, while the *Renown* & *Ark Royal* were within 1,000 miles, so the Hun had either to run the Allied gauntlet, resign herself to being interned at Montevideo or do what she eventually did, come out & scuttle herself. This important happening coincided with the torpedoing of a German cruiser by one of our submarines and the scuttling of the 33,000 tonne *Colombia* of the Norddeutscher Line in mid Atlantic—altogether excellent material for a stinging

(41)   Churchill broadcast, nor was it wasted.

'Z' received its new carburettor, but did not return suitable thanks to its maker and about one or two revolutions per se, remained cold and motionless like a museum piece. And Gore himself plus hoodoo continued to give amusement to all but himself. C'est ça as Forster would say, c'est la Guerre as the French would say, but what is it really?

'A' Flight 615 flew across to St Inglevert to act as escort to the leave ships, but on the 19th one of their pilots crashed and was killed so hurried arrangements [...] were made for our Flight to go across the next day and relive them.

The morning of the 20th was brightened by some low flying and straffing of the troops along the Arras–Douai road by flights of Battles & Blenheims. At lunch-time we learned that one section of 'B' Flight was to reinforce us. After lunch Red Section, Gore, Blackadder, [and] Radcliffe, and Yellow, Kayll, Irving, [and] Forster, took off, and soon after their arrival at St Inglevert, Green Section, Bazin, Hawkes, [and] Humpherson, also turned up. Refuelling was carried out

(42)   quickly as at last we ran into a reasonable petrol pump. There were two hangars, one used by the French to house their Breugets: these machines used for Army Co-Op are some ten years old and look it; the other is shared by us & the French transport; we got several machines in and picketed two out. One broke its tailwheel unit. We spent a good hour with the French awaiting the coming of our two lorries, both arrived together despite having left at 1½ hour interval. We saw our airmen safely billeted in a large bell tent with plenty of straw and five wooden twinbeds at the village of Wadenthun about one Km to the East of the aerodrome: Flt Sgt B-A had a very decent room also in the village at 5 francs a night: they fed at a pub some 300 yards from the aerodrome, La Miraills [*sic*], where for 31 francs a day they got three quite solid meals. The officers were several Kms away by the sea at Wissant, Hotel des Baines [Hôtel des Bains]: a good pub which gave us a very good

(43)   and welcome dinner: clean rooms with running water—cold. The French Arme De La Air [Armée De L'Air] living at the Hotel Belleview [Bellevue] further up the village. And so to bed.

Gravstad was supposed to be coming with us, but after a tremendous black in Lille the evening before, when he failed to make the last train or apparently any effort to return home, the CO confined him to camp pending his pleasure.

We closed down for the night little less wise as to why and what, but we hoped for news in the morning.

Thursday, December 21st–Wednesday, December 27th

[Entered up the side:] Destroyer telling RAF in words to go away as if we would understand.

The morning brought both news and fun—lots of fun. We were up and coffee consumed by 6.15 but no lorry: a clear starry sky. About 6.45 lorry turned up and we chased along more or less up hill and down dale into St Inglevert. News came that tow sections were to escort the leave boat departing from Boulogne at 7.30 am while one section was to remain at the base at

(44)   five minutes' readiness: Foster's machine being U/S, Kayll took Hawkes' Blue machine. A thick mist had come down, and we skimmed the tree tops on our way to the coast: both sections picked up the leave boat, on which our C.O was said to be travelling, and along with the Anson and

a destroyer, helped it on its way. As the ceiling was 3/400 feet this called for care, so Anson—Yellow—did left-hand and Red right-hand circuits: even so Will Gore as mathematician in Chief was out to show that they were bound to meet and it required the grace of Providence to save them from the consequences. After escorting the ship 10 miles on its way we said goodbye—without any flourish—and returned to seek out our base in the mist. Kayll's sound navigation saw to this, but the Almighty had to be called on once more. […] The next five minutes were all crammed full of excitement for all, but soberly state this is what happened: Kayll seeing the aerodrome gave Yellow echelon right

(45)   exit, Hawkes into the mist of which more anon. Gore, presuming Yellow would land first smack, cut across the corner against the circuit and met face to face with Kayll who passed the Vic on its left; Irving, who dived below, actually touched down in the field. Gore then gave Red echelon right, & exit Harry, who luckily caught sight of Blackadder as the latter went round again [added in pencil:](and made rude darts at him). So Harry landed—urgently for his tailwheel and our mainwheel were broken. There remained John Hawkes: he was given instructions to land at Boulogne but 10 mins later a Gladiator skimmed across the aerodrome, landed, took off & landed once more happily on his second effort—to wit Hawkes and with not a map in his possession; apparently he lost Kayll in the echelon & did not realise he was so near the aerodrome, so flew a course to the sea, hit Cap Gris Nez and followed the shore along to Wissent [Wissant], where he picked up the Hotel des Bains and so back along our bus route, though not before additional worry had fallen on him through picking

(46)   the wrong road at a junction, which brought him back to the sea. However Ende Gut, alles gut, and an unusual hearty breakfast was enjoyed, while Harry visited his cousin with greater care thereafter. His long hair on end after landing will be a memory souvenir of the occasion.

An excellent lunch was had at our hotel of hors d'oeuvres (shrimps, eel and pâté) Pumphrey turned up in 'F' after lunch & brought the news that Doctor David had at last come having spent only four days en route. Gore, Forster & Radcliffe flew on a reconnaissance of the coastal Sector and after their return the readiness Section [of] Kayll, Blackadder, [and] Irving were ordered to take off & investigate the gunfire that had been reported over Calais; fortunately Bazin ignored this & it proved that Seclin had been informed by the St Inglevert wireless corporal that there was 'heavy' gunfire so ordered us off & also a Section of Hurricanes from Le Touquet. Actually there

(47)   were only a few bursts, & when told this, the order was immediately cancelled, just in time for us, but too late for the Hurri buses. Encore une fois c'est la presume! Taken all in all it was quite an exciting first day. The night also was not without incident, as the lorry with spare parts arrived at midnight at Wissant and there were loud shouts from Kayll: Forster was […] having one of his nights off, anyway he got Joe up and a very secret letter of instructions was handed over, dated Ca va Sans dine two days before.

The second day was less eventful, but even so we managed to break a few more tailwheels so that at one time only four machines out of ten were serviceable, however the repair service was good and altogether more hours were flown than the previous day. The weather was perfect, cold and strong sunshine rather like [in] Switzerland, and the ceiling was limitless. Blackadder only followed by Gore & Pumphrey succeeded in chasing a machine bats out up the Channel, which turned out to be an air

(48)   liner with 'Belgique' written across its fuselage in enormous letters, coloured bright red.

Cpl Gaskin and eight airmen from 'B' Flight had arrived the evening before and arrangements were made to billet them in a barn on straw but they had brought beds with them, so should be comfortable and La Mirrailles [*sic*] price was brought down to 28 francs a day.

The reply to our invitation to the French Armée de l'Air to dine with us one evening was that they would be delighted to do so on the 26th if we could honour them on the 23rd, so that, combined with the party we propose for our troops on the 24th and our own affair on the 25th, […] the Xmas festivities [should be covered] pretty adequately.

The Frenchmen's home aerodrome is at Montpellier between Marseilles and the Pyrenees, and they complain bitterly of the cold.

The third day the sky was clear from dawn to dusk and from 7.30 until close at 2 pm a constant patrol was maintained, altogether 25 hours were flown, which was good going, as several of our 10 machines were U/S.

(49)   Several pursuits were undertaken, but either it was a friendly or neutral aircraft. The number of broken tailwheels continued to mount up, and last night 'F's went, when being pushed into the hanger of all things.

Doctor David, our mystery man, at last turned up, once again overdue. He arrived in nice time for our own party with the French at the Hotel Bellevue, and then excelled with vivid descriptions of the castrating punishment he thought should be the lot of all Germans, descriptions which the French acclaimed. And his 'bitches' references likewise went down well.

However as a party it was not up to the standard set at previous functions: the fare was wholesome and the wines ordinary; besides we were all very tired since in addition to the flying we had been kept at readiness until 5.50. In fact one section was all set for taking off: Kayll, Gore & W.F.B. and remained at 30 minutes, all night. At lunch Will Gore had delighted his neighbours who were revolted by the garlic in the meat

(50)   by his references to an appalling night—journey in summer 3rd class on a French train in a carriage filled with overflowing garlic—smelling hommes and both windows closed as "It's all useful experience," followed by a suck from his pipe.

David's journey had also been an experience: he was ordered to report at Southampton; a bad crossing to Cherbourg followed and then railway trains all over France with an itinerary that included Paris, Amiens, Arras and Vitry before coming on to St Inglevert by lorry, itself a good four hours run.

Xmas eve there was no flying, also thick mist covered the ground all day. Doctor having awakened visited the men's billets and declared they were insanitary, so a sticker was put up to Group with the result that permission was obtained to find billets for them elsewhere preferably Wisent [Wissant]. The Hotel des Bains was the solution, for they were able to supply rooms for all at the very reasonable price of five francs per day. Linen included, but the men

(51)   to look after their own quarters. It was intended to hold a party in Boulogne, but the mist was on the ground and it was obviously going to be a hell of a journey, so we stayed chez nous and went to bed early—soon to be awakened by a plausible rendering of Noel and Blaydon races [Geordie folk songs] by our men at midnight.

[Entered up the side:] Men sick in ???????'s car.

Christmas day weather was no improvement on its predecessor, and it was not long before we were allowed two sections released and one at 30 mins. Doc, Bazin & W.F.B. went into Calais where Bazin's long enduring quest for liquid paraffin had its journeys end. The rest of us drilled the troops on the aerodrome and tried to make em' repent of their misconduct—not one had turned up in time for the lorry, and one had sicked himself en route to St Ing. [St Inglevert]. Altogether an unfortunate beginning to the day of goodwill. Before we lunched, we went down to the shore and fooled about on the sands: after lunch that procedure was repeated except, this time organised four-a-side football with bare feet was attempted—the mermaids Kayll (?), Bazin, Irving, Forster played a draw 3–3 with the beach-lions Gore,

(52)   Blackadder, Pumphrey & Radcliffe, but needless to say there was a complete shambles before the end. However good was done and we were all to enjoy our tea at the hotel and to make a rather brave effort at solving a jig saw puzzle. [Entered up the side:] Harry Noel

The first airmen arrived soon after 7 pm and we were able to sit down to table half an hour later than arranged, Kayll at the head of our table & Doc David presiding the other. We had two officers facing each other at various parts of each table, with airmen clustered around. We had half arranged for the party to end at 10, but actually it was not long before midnight when our guests took their leave. The decorations were simple but effective. Two blue & white streamers, holly round the lights, four bottles with candles on each table, two candlesticks burning by the mirror, […] a few Xmas cards on the mantelpiece [and] in the centre […] the one of the King & Queen sent to us by them. The repas itself was a success, oxtail soup, cod, turkey with brussels sprouts, potatoes and stuffing, Crème Chantilly which was very popular, mandarins & nuts and coffee. Drinks

(53)   were confined to French beer, whose alcoholic content was fortunately negligible. Cigars and cigarettes. Kayll proposed the health of the King in addition to the opening 'Thank God'. Doc David raised his glass to sweethearts, wives and absent friends, and in reply to his own toast made the following sentimental ovation in French. "Merci beaucoup, mais pourquoi ja sans tris heureux de cette manifestation." And no French scholar could have improved on it. After the meal one of the 'B' Flight airmen Storey took his seat at the piano and he and Green amused the company: but the highlight of the evening was 'A' Flight song, composed by Story and Wright. It started off to the strain of 'Heigh Ho' from Snow White, the actual words were to the tune of 'Uncle Tom Cobly & All', while it ended with 'A Merry Christmas To You':

Joe Kayll, Joe Kayll, hand me an old kite,
All away out, along down, along lea,
To do this patrol on a cold winter night,
With: (CHORUS)

Snow-white [H.P.R.], Grumpy Gore, Bashful Irving, Sneezy Dixon, Doc Pumphrey, Sleepy Forster, Happy Blackadder and all.

(54)

Grumpy Gore, Grumpy Gore your guns are all right,
All along out, along down, along lea,

Although they freeze up at a hell of a height,
With ———

Doc Pumphrey, Doc Pumphrey, your radio's dead,
All along out, all along down, along lea,
You'd better come down & let's all go to bed,
With ———

Blackadder, Blackadder, Oh! Put her down light,
All along out, all along down, along lea,
or another tailwheel will have gone for a shite,
With ———

Snow White, Snow White, you've lost your way,
All along out, all along down, along lea,
We'll put the clock back another day,
[reference to H.P.R.s made after our effort that he had forgotten to put his
clock back & expected another hour's daylight]
With ———

Joe Kayll, Joe Kayll, now the fog has come down,
All along out, all along down, along lea,
You won't be happy till the kites are washed down,
With ———

Joe Kayll, Joe Kayll, your kite is alright,
All along out, all along down, along lea,
For B.A.s had us working by day and by night,
With ———

Here's to Doc Smith, for now we're content,
All along out, all along down, along lea,
If it weren't for him we'd be in a tent,
WITHOUT———

(55)   Blackadder proposed the health of Barret Atkinson & 'A' Flight
airmen wi so [*sic*]:

Here's to Flight Sergeant
And his men in blue
He chose them well, he chose them true

B.A. his name, but B.A. not they
No better crowd will you find today.

Boxing day was another wash out from flying, so we all ambled along the beach towards the hill with the monument. In the evening eleven French officers came to dine: we were only ten as Milne Irving—now a proud father—had pushed off by road with John Sample, who paid us a fleeting visit. M.M.I goes on leave on the 28th so it was deemed wise to make sicca [produce tears]. The evening's party was slow starting, affected no doubt by the sluggish way in which the various courses made their appearance. However the Frenchmen with their singing—anything from a powerful solo rendering of The Pagliacci [Italian opera] to a theme song of Provence sung by all—and Humpherson with his guitar, ably supported by Will Gore and his voice but feebly backed by the rest of us until the popular 'Old grey Mare' was called upon, did eventually get the party going. And it was just one step further to games. First Kayll demonstrated the

(56)   art of catching a falling stick and our [?] friends showed themselves very good pupils. Cock Fighting went to us, also hoorie woorie round a wee baton then a run, but at the team boat-race, after two long and epic struggles, France prevailed. Their novelties consisted of:

(i) A race from our end of the room to the other with a lighted candle.
(ii) Sitting on an empty champagne bottle with a lighted candle on one side and an unlit one on the other, you had to take the lighted candle and light the other one, then return both to their respective places.
(iii) An old favourite; blindfolding a man who stands on a board and places his hands outwardly to steady himself—on another fellows head. The latter goes full knee bend, the plank is raised with difficulty a couple of inches, then the victim is told to jump.

John Hawkes gave a perfect exhibition. When the Allied party had spent itself, Radcliffe and Kayll organised a ball, which quickly terminated as Pah-rez laid hold on the one lass that could pass the lesson.
    December 27th—we flew on the two

(57)   patrols until lunch when 615 Sections relieved us; however Greens came upon a mine, so had to keep up a continuous patrol over it until naval vessels came to investigate. As a result 'A' Flight were able to fly back to Vitry, but 'B' Flight had to wait until the next day.

Thursday, December 28th–Friday, January 12th [1940]

We had our first fall of snow overnight, and not only the ground but our machines were thickly covered when we arrived at the terrain. After removing the layer from the bottom mainplane Joe took off on a test flight, which went off satis though the machine was somewhat loath to leave the ground at first.

Blackadder went off by lorry to St Inglevert and after two days returned with 'F'. He did see this Heinkel which Saunders (615) had chased from zero to 23,000 ft and eventually opened fire; the Heinkel had gone into a steep dive, but whether this was evasive action or a mortal plunge evidence was lacking. Altogether 615 appeared to be having a much more eventful time than we had, what with enemy machines and mines.

(58) Meanwhile George White was fast becoming a French scholar and won a fierce exchange with a taxi driver with the final words: 'nous vous fayer comme nous arrive'.

On the 31st the rest of our troops arrived from home and Vitry is now lousy with the RAF.

W.F.B., Pumphrey, Forster and Plinston, the new F/O attached to our Flight, went into Lille to give the New Year a rousing welcome and succeeded. Blackadder also managed to dislocate his thumb after, but from all accounts falls were not rare. Their taxi deposited them home at 5 am after a dirty journey through fog and Pumphrey immediately showed it was very easy to ground on the home field as on the away. He continued the good work next morning or rather three hours later when he eventually awoke. About 11 pm The Under Secretary of State for Air, Captain Harold Balfour, arrived by car, accompanied by our A.O.C. Air Vice Marshal Blount, and Air Vice Marshal Douglas, with the Assistant Chief of the Air Staff and several other RAF and military. He had a look at the fabric on F and put his finger

(59) through it with ease, then came across to the Nissen hut where we were presented. He confirmed that both the Squadrons are to be re equipped with Hurricanes very shortly.

The weather became bitterly cold and one night 26 degrees of frost was reported: certainly there was a layer of ice in the water pumps and even hair oil, while sponges were like pieces of pumice stone and the sides of one's basin were lagged with icicles. Our machines fared no happier than their pilots and infinite patience was required to start them. One morning we were not able to report at 5 minutes readiness until 11.30, over four hours behind time. And frost covered all the fabric, the controls were iced up, and icicles were hanging from several places. All in all decidedly unpleasant weather on the ground, but quite agreeable for flying.

(60)   [Reference to Radcliffe entered up the side:] Flew reciprocal after course to Amiens had brought him slap bang over Cathedral.

On Tuesday, January 2nd, Harry Radcliffe staked yet another claim to the Forced Landing Trophy, when he erred from the straight and narrow on the return half of a cross-country to Amiens and being rather dubious as to his then present whereabouts landed in a field some five miles to the South East of Lille and approaching the Belgian frontier. Once again the landing was effected with unsurpassed dexterity, no damage was done and Joe Kayll appeared to have little difficulty in flying it out the following day. The great man returned home shortly after his machine and at once assured his fellow pilots that he was not going to say anything for he knew already of their disbelief—however the story was not long in leaking out, improving at every chapter until finally   […] presented to the CO it was a masterpiece. In conclusion a remark of Tony Forster's, while the CO & Harry were pacing the turf, is worth recording: 'look at Harry—he's got his best bullshitting face on.' What do you mean? On the evening of the 3rd Wing Co Eccles, C'O., Sample, Doc David, White, Humph, W.F.B. & Forster dined at the Hotel Moderne in Arras before continuing to the theatre to see the NAAF I show with Will Fyfe in the lead. Most excellent entertainment. Maskerlin the Magician,

(61)   Robert Wilson to sing Scottish and other songs, and three dancing lovelies, whose bellies were soon blackened from the dirt of the stage floor and of course Will Fyfe himself, 'O' I belong to Glasgow! Belch.' Did the Padre hear that? (Group Capt Keen, sponsor of the show) 'it's all right, Sir, it's all right. That was only an echo from the valley of content'. After the show the Group Capt chased us round behind, the first into his dressing room, & he shook hands very warmly, saying he was just thinking of joining the ballroom barrage (ref belly outsize). We were under the impression we were to be offered a drink, but Fyfe remarked 'there are too many of you, so you'll just have to watch me drink'.

On the 4th we had a visit from Wing Co Livingston, the eye expert, who demonstrated a pair of the new goggles with which we were shortly to be supplied—they looked excellent & their field of vision much better than anything previously produced. But at £4 a piece they otto be good.

(62)   A heated discussion at tea time over the possible development of the war with particular reference to the war in the air. Drem was held up as an example of complete disorganisation. Where in the words of

Bobbie Pumphrey 'You saw Group Captains running about like frightened chickens.' Our own Wing Co overheard the sentence without noticeable pleasure.

But the chief job at the moment is 'The affair of 607 Orderly room' of yesterday. Our CO had informed Cooper that he intended to promote him to corporal. The sergeant cook had forgotten to dish out the main issue the evening before. This is the background to the story. By putting the two together, it followed easily that at midday on the 3rd Cooper decided to celebrate his promotion (so gave it out at lunch the following day). Fried chicken & he joined forces, dared their rightful men, then proceeded to attack anybody else's men they could pretend to sign away. After that Cooper later admitted that he had put back a full pint [from the] services menu, they proceeded

(63)   to a cafe haunt of theirs, had four Pernods and a coffee. George White encountered Cooper at the door and thought he was looking more bright than usual but he answered intelligently. George went up to his room and some minutes later heard Cooper being more forceful than customary. 'You get on with it. It's 607 that counts. To Hell with Wing.' More minutes passed then unmistakeable sounds of illness were heard. George rushed across & found Crickmore being supported with sick all over his clothes. He was helped downstairs to the telephone room. George returned to his room to find out what's what. But it had been too much for Cooper & he was sicking himself like a gentleman in the yard, when he was surprised by the CO. The latter took one look then dashed upstairs with a very pale face, and burst in on George. What on earth am I to do? Cooper's dead drunk. A wild noise was heard from below and Crickmore speaking voluble French. It was decided to send him to Sick Quarters

(64)   and he was escorted out but he collapsed in the street. So the ambulance was summoned and off he went on a stretcher. David now enters the stage, for he heard an unusual noise in his den. Entering he saw an airman vaguely familiar, with hair dishevelled and glasses away sicking into an empty petrol tin. He asked him his name [and was answered] 'Crishmo ssh' (Crickmore Sir), [who] promptly emphasised it with renewed pewings. And in the meanwhile a very miserable Cooper with one hand on the door handle and the other against the wall for support was facing the C.O, and having a hell of a strip torn off without [...] G.C.W. understanding a word that was being said. Altogether the best show since the war began.

The following story appears in A.M. Weekly Intelligence Summary, 30.1x. 39: 'The pride of German pilots has been shaken by two incidents during the past few weeks'—one somewhere in England. The pilot was

(65)   a German, brought down near our coast. When he was dragged from the aircraft and asked if he were hurt, he answered in English with an Elizabethan flavour: 'Not physically, but morally. To be shot down by a bloody biplane piloted by a bloody barrister is more than I can bloody well bear.'—[according to] Dudley Craig.

On the 5th a sudden thaw set in and the remaining patches of snow quickly disappeared. With the change in temperature came bad weather and low cloud and very poor visibility, so non-operational flying which had been at a standstill on account of the hardness of the ground and the consequent danger to tailwheel units, remained at a standstill. However incidents still happened. One most unfortunate involved Wearmouth, who was seriously burned when his clothes caught fire from some petrol in our Nissan hut: Joe Kayll fortunately was there and managed to extinguish the flames, but a lot of damage had been done.

Churchill paid his Squadron a visit of some ten minutes on the 9th but unfortunately most of them were still weatherbound at St Inglevert: he evinced no desire to see us, although

(66)   we were all ready for him. The day before a press representative accompanied by Sq Ldr Smart had been shown round by W.F.B., who however had first committed the appalling blunder of mistaking two officers of the Buffs for the press.

All preparations were made to leave for St Ing [St Inglevert] at 2.45pm but of course they came to nought: however the next day we did at last get away. Red Section, Blackadder, Dixon, [and] Bowen, went first, had lunch at Wissant and were able to do the afternoon patrol. 'B' Flight with Sample, Hawkes, Whitty, Plinston, Thompson and Stewart had meanwhile arrived while our two new Ford vans with Pumphrey and Flt Lt Fidler (the armament officer ex 60 Wing) were not long in following.

Only two patrols were carried out on the 11th and nothing seen. The CO & Doc Crombie arrived by road in the afternoon and joined the evening party at Boulogne: we bathed at the Hotel Maurice before going on to the Restaurant Excelsior for a very indifferent meal. Clear sky and hard frost once again, so the aerodrome is now more or less u/s for other than operational flying until it thaws or a new supply of tailwheel

(67)   units arrives. On the 12th one or two aircraft were reported and machines despatched to intercept but with results nil. Fidler & W.F. B. Carried out a practice to test the efficiency of searchlights as indicators in daylight.

Saturday, January 13th–Wednesday, February 7th

While on patrol A ex Cap Gris Nez, Red Section (W.F.B., H.P.R., R.E.W.P.) sighted a wisp of cloud forming high above them. W.F.B. detached himself and set off in pursuit; while climbing up, two thinner lines of cloud were seen to approach the thicker line and break off abruptly on reaching it: then the attacked machine did a steep right turn and dived down, and disappeared into the haze. The two thinner lines proved to be our Curtiss friends whom we had met at Norrent Fortes and they apparently did what was needed, for the enemy was compelled to land, in a field not far from the Calais Marck aerodrome. It proved to be a Dornier 215 [original entry is 'Dornier 17' but '215' was later added above this in pencil] and its crew of three were made prisoner: it had touched down with its wheels lowered, but they had collapsed on coming against a ditch. Even so, little damage was

(68) done and the French military were on the crew before they had time to destroy anything. The Captain actually was about to tear up his map on which were marked all the objectives he had set out to photograph, but it was snatched from him.

The CO phoned up the Commandant at Marck [*sic*] and obtained permission for a party of us to go and inspect the machine the following morning. So at 7.00 hours off went the Hillman van with Plinston, Bazin, Blackadder, Hawkes, Pumphrey, Dixon, Whitty and Stewart. We were the first 'visitors' to arrive, but while we were, many others rolled up. We met the Lieut [Lieutenant] who had taken the Boch prisoner. What stunned us most about the Dornier was its smallness, though if we had consulted our tablets we would have found its wing-span was less than 60ft. Almost equally surprising was its complete lack of armament, though there were fittings in the engines for a couple of canons: the Hun had concentrated entirely on his cameras, and carries four really cracking affairs. Altogether there would be about forty bullets in the machine, several of which had gone through the engine while there was a nasty burst near the cockpit. The instruments

(69) were also high class, and the machine was equipped with three compasses alone.

Afterwards we went to Marck aerodrome and had a look at some Potez 63 reconnaissance and Bloch 131 light bombers: we also inspected the two Curtiss Hawks which had taken part in the combat: each machine had but one shot at least through its prop—one was armed with six, the other with four guns.

We had coffee at the Faison Gris in Calais, and some of us stayed; books of doubtful taste were purchased, R.E.W.P. drank himself, while M.H.B.T. had refused to believe that brothels in France could close at 9.30 pm.

And two stories came to light: one re J.R.H. on his honeymoon, [who] slept in a 1st class sleeper between Newcastle and London. At a crucial moment the noise of a passing train was heard, whence No. 1 sat up and exclaimed: "Oh! That must be the 10.30, its two minutes late." The other historie, more topical, refers to the current fear of a German invasion of Holland–Belgium. Bubbly Bowen, alias Popeye, in reply to [the] remark 'This flap seems to have quietened

(70)   down a bit,' came out with the gem: 'Oh! Yes, it went off in the Hillman at 8 o' clock'—at the same hour the CO left St Inglevert by road for Vitry to go into conference with George.

On the 15th Red Section (W.F.B., H.P.D., Fidler) repeated its experiences of two days before. This time W.F.B. sighted the trail of smoke a few minutes before the patrol was due to end so he took the whole section off in pursuit. The trail led towards St Omer and had meanwhile been attacked by two thinner trails: over St Omer, there appeared to be a wow, then the big trail was seen to be streaking along the Belgian Frontier towards Calais and the sea. The smaller trails—for even at 17,000ft it was impossible to pick out the machines—were still mobbing the larger trail, when they broke away as their petrol was running short and searched for the aerodrome in the thick haze.

The morning of the 16th was distinguished by the failure of the lorry taking No. 1 detail

(71)   to the aerodrome [...] to get more than half way up the hill outside Hervelinghen and [it] promptly returned to the bottom more or less out of control but fortunately without accident. As a result we had to walk the remaining 1½ kms and missed our first patrol.

The Low Countries scare is supposed to have eased but the French are still very excited, and more busses carrying troops towards the Belgian Frontier passed the aerodrome last night while on our Wissant road there are some busses drawn up at the side—waiting.

Shortly after Red Section had landed from the afternoon patrol, a tremendous blizzard set in and reduced visibility to a few yards: our troops pushing the aircraft into the hangar were soon covered in white, and Rigger Stewart remarked 'Finland be fucked!' And at tea friend Bazin came out with an equally worthy remark, addressed to Bowen: 'The two minutes silence must upset you a lot.'

The next incident in our life of detachment was the renewal of leave, so exit Johnnie Sample

(72)   and then on January 19th followed a morning of intense cold: the thermometer was registering 27° of frost, when we pushed out our machines at 7am and the wind was bitter. Only two would start, but they were never called upon to perform after the early patrol.

On the 20th we all drove into Boulogne for a bath at the Meurice and the French version of 'The Lion Has Wings', which could have been a lot worse; we dined at the Meurice and some of us danc[ing] in the room below ran into Harry O'Brian of Richmond, one of the many Army officers spending the night there before going on leave. A filthy drive back in a sweeping blizzard.

The wind was blowing hard next am and there would be about 6″ of snow, besides considerable drifts. Decided weather was unfit for flying, after F had stuck itself in the middle of the aerodrome and had to be brought back as much under man as horse power. The old Francis when chasing the Hillman solemnly disappeared from view into a snowdrift and had to be more or

(73)   less dug out. Bobbie Pumphrey still a-bed with his sore throat, and others threatening to follow his example. More diggings-out were necessary as the day wore on, for the snow drifted across the roads ever deeper and deeper. At one stage of the procedures both our lorries were missing, with all our men on board: however they had only got stuck and the Frenchmen pulled them out. The Hillman was sent into Boulogne to collect Wing Co Eccles fresh from leave and it must have been about the best vehicle to make the journey: certainly in the afternoon when the Wing C tried to visit the aerodrome; he got hopelessly stuck and the car had to be released with picks and shovels: drifts now fully 4 to 5 feet. His own car coming from Vitry made Calais successfully but had to be abandoned half way to St Inglevert and the unfortunate driver had to plough 10kms through the snow. Many mines were washed up on the shore, one suspiciously Teutonic in appearance which was zealously but inadequately grounded by the French military. We invited our A.O.C. to dine with us at the Hotel and while we were playing 'Tippet' there was a vivid flash followed by a land explosion and the tinkling of shattered glass.

(74)   We hurried through the blizzard to the shore expecting to view chaos and perhaps bodies but all that was to be seen was deep snow right up to the water's edge; whether it was the Tenton [*sic*] or not we could not tell, but indications were that it was a newly beached mine that had exploded.

Comic relief—a story of yesterday. John Hawkes rang up Parey for a weather report, and a cheerful voice answered 'You don't really want one do you?' 'I do,' whereon a report was sent over at Ribbentrop speed, so John asked for a repeat. "Visibility—one thousand at fifteen hundred yards." "Yes, visibility 1,000—1,500 yds. Silly, wasn't it?" And John's cup of mirth overflowed.

We have got a most pompous address with the formation of a new group in the establishment of separate RAF Command in France. It reads:

No. 607 Squadron
Auxiliary Air Force
61 Fighter Wing
14 Group
BAF
BEF
France.

And so we are no longer a mere Servicing Unit!

4

Diary of William Francis Blackadder

Part Two

Saturday, January 13th–Wednesday, February 7th

(75)   Days of extreme idleness followed, as the aerodrome was pronounced unserviceable on account of the depth of the snow, however we looked upon it as a duty to put in an appearance. So each day a small party of officers and men struggled through nobly looked around and returned. Eventually on the afternoon of the 28th flying was resumed when WFB took off for the Gris Nez patrol. But restrictions on flying are greater than ever: sections are to be of one machine only and there is to be no flying other than operational, so it looks as though we shall shortly be adept at twiddling our thumbs—we certainly ought to be by now.

With this pronounced lack of activity, tongues are wagging and summonses rife. Needless to say the Hurricanes have not yet arrived, but there is talk of going back to Blighty to re-equip. The alternative would appear to be a visit to the aerodrome near Rouen. There was also talk of the entire Squadron moving to Le Touquet, but as 85 appear to have made the position there untenable, so if the Squadron does move, it will probably be to St Inglevert.

Weather is still bitterly cold, testified

(76)   by the frequent appearances of flights of wild geese over head. And the cold seems to be getting most of the chaps down, and there is much minor sickness, chiefly sore throats.

On the 31st WFB took the train to base and returned two days later with the latest scandal, which was considerable. Flap featured first and foremost, and there was little definite news either of our future movements or aircraft. During his [WFB's] absence a pronounced thaw set in, and in a few days most of the snow had melted and transferred roads into rivers, notably our special road.

We were all set for leaving on Feb 4th but the Wing Co would not have it, as it was already too late in the day: instead permission was obtained for one machine to fly and several members of 'A' Flight disgraced themselves with exhibitions of low flying. 'F' fires m.g.s out to sea over Hotel Des Baines [Hôtel des Bains].

A few days later we had our first real exercise since crossing the Channel, when ten officers played ten-a-side football against ten airmen on the sands for over 100 minutes, until eventually the officers were leading by 7 goals to 5.

(77)   With the rapid thaw the roads had begun to cut up badly, so it came as no surprise when the French authorities put a ban on all heavy vehicles. This meant of course that we were marooned at St Inglevert, a situation not altogether unpleasant, but Hawkes was pining for base where letter deliveries were regular. Craig came up to relieve him.

February 8th–February 19th

WFB on leave, so little known of the Flight's activities apart from a really shocking effort in Lille with courant to the fore [*sic*]. For leave the common practice has been to spend the night at the Hotel Maurice [Meurice] in Boulogne and so save a deadly journey in a train at snail's speed. The boat crossed to Dover with an escort of a destroyer and if the weather permits an Anson and a section of Flight aircraft. Before going on board you receive your ration card which is generous in its allowances: at Dover the customs examination is extremely superficial for Officers practically non-existent, and the boat-load is emptied into the waiting train

(78)   within half an hour. At London you each go your own way by normal passenger train, though there are special buses waiting at Victoria to take you across to the other main line stations if you wish. Coming back you have to report to the R.T.O. at Victoria at a set hour, and frequently you have to spend the night at Dover on account of an early morning sailing. Officers put up at the Lord Warden hotel, and get their bed and breakfast for half a crown. And so to Boulogne and from there special troop trains to the bigger towns.

On leave WFB visited Usworth and encountered James Vick, Minnie Manton and Leslie Runciman. Usworth was all upside down and bad weather had held the work up for six weeks, so it will be some time before it is serviceable. Wing Co Fanny Adams is still in charge, and among his

(79)   entourage are to be found Dob Wardale browned-off on the whole, Cabbie Hanson still no doubt handing over, Cocky Wild who was cheered at the information that we had picked up his voice on the R/T, and of course many of the others such as Saul etc., while Norman and Maine still wait upon them, though Coles has received the sack. Taken all in all it was not the Usworth of old and certainly not an Auxiliary Mess.

There had been some excitement the day before, when Sq Ldr Shute & a section of 152 had come upon a Heinkel and apparently experienced little difficulty in putting their petite biplanes into such a position as to overcome the enemy. But a few days later one heard they were being re-equipped with Spitfires, so Higher Command must not have been as impressed as mons [*sic*] aunties.

James Vick had not received command of 609 after all, as he had

(80)   been placed unfit for flying duties. So instead he was limping as a Sq Ldr [of] Ops at Tangmere and was not pleased. Neither was Manton, who was longing for a Squadron but who was still marking time at Air Ministry; he had news of Singer, who was back in this country living in London.

Our H.A.C. was in good form, and very pleased as the C.A.S. had smiled upon his proposal to visit his Squadron in the field; his latest toy was an illustration of a practice known in Shipping circles as de-gaussing: two Dops, magnetic, which display a remarkable affection in timely doplike manner.

Monday, February 19th–Saturday, March 24th

Will Gore is now mourning the loss of 'Z', for his tough sparring partner was written off at St Inglevert: it cut out when Dudley Craig was taking off on patrol and was

(81)   not very badly damaged when he force-landed successfully in a wee field, but evil—though perhaps they were good—forces got to work and by the time the last gentleman had called to inspect the body, she was very sick and pronounced unfit for any work in the future: soon after she died and the body was reliably dismembered by kites, both officers and airmen. R.I.P.

During our detachment the remainder of the Flight had done good work: Will Gore and party had dug a refuge hole near our Nissen hut, while Dame Nature had done equally well and made several cavities all over the place; the best bit of work had been put into the finishing & embellishing of our hut and it was now extremely comfortable—much more so than the Mess: a partition between Officers and airmen's quarters was a great improvement as it means we now had some sort of privacy.

(82)   On Saturday February 24th, the H.A.C. arrived by air and was suitably met: in the evening he was taken by road into Lille and contact was established at the Métropole with Blackadder & Pumphrey two hours after the allotted time, hours which the two of the advance party had whiled away with Cardinal Puff aux Champagne cocktails. Dinner was held chez Madame Audri and we sat down to table as follows.

(83)   Pumphrey, Rutherford, Humpherson

Thompson	Kayll
Parrott	Runciman
Graeme	Blackadder
Dixon	

Forster, D.A. Smith, L.E. Smith

Regrettable absentees: Bazin, Craig, Hawkes.
Absent in Paris: Sample, Gore.
Absent on leave: White, Whitty, etc.

We dined well and long, and Madame displayed becoming attention to notre général, who in return produced his performing oaps [*sic*] for her. Altogether it was a successful party and we were warm within when we wandered without: in the square two vehicles stood at our disposal; the CO elected to drive the Hillman, so we all came home in the Comma; en route several regrettable incidents occurred, redeemed perhaps by the overpowering friendship of the Medical Officer for the unfortunate Blackadder, who was in ill condition to reciprocate.

(84)   Next day 25% of our strength Officers and men were given authority to travel to Paris to see a British Army XV play France. Those that remained got up [...] at a later hour, as Summertime had been introduced. The H.A.C. elected to fly a Magister with WFB as navigator but they had no sooner taken off than a sudden flap swept over the aerodrome and a hasty QBI landing had to be made. Taxying was even worse and Bazin discovered them steering a westerly course, and called them back to safety. H.A.C. talked at length and had tea in the 'A' Flight hut. While we went across to 'B' Flight for lunch to taste of the poached partridges, the gibrir

[*sic*] of one Bazin, whose exploits 'à la chasse rival those of the celebrated Tartarin. The weather did not improve much, so H.A.C. continued his journey to Rheims by road.

On the 26th the Wing played its first game of rugby football, when thanks to some good operating by Tony, fifteen men under the leadership of WFB turned up to oppose a

(85)   local detachment of the RAs; after a hard struggle lasting thirty minutes each way on a very soft pitch, the opposition emerged victorious by a solitary goal scored shortly before full time; by no stretch of the imagination could we be called a good side, considering the previous training had been absolutely zero we might have performed a lot worse; a special mention should be made of Tony, Bobbie and Montie who arrived back from Paris at 4.30 am & gone up straight away to the Nissen hut & and who now endured an hour's agony in silence. The team was: Sq Ldr L. E. Smith REWP; M.H.R.T; LAC Wing; A.D.F. & PO Collard; PO Hope, WFB, PO Parrott, PO Paxton, F/O Irving, J.R.K., Cpl Spanton, Keen. There was no fraternisation after the game as we had neither car nor baths, so each player had to sort for himself.

However two days later there was fraternisation when the CO WFB Sq Ldr Tremlett, Flt Lt Saunders, [and] PO Fredman (latter two of 615) went to Cambrai and lunched with the French Squadron: after the usual three hours of eating, drinking, singing, button exchanging and

(86)   plate and window breaking (from which mark you L.E.S. restrained himself) they went along to the aerodrome and watched a sous Officer throw a Morane about like a piece of paper; some fine flick rolls both on the level and upwards. A pleasant, comfortable machine with two mitrailleuses and a canon firing through the prop but with a magazine of only 60 shells: does 450 KPS so is not fast enough & they will shortly be re-equipped with the new Dewoitine. One of their young POs had been awarded the Croix de Guerre (nouveau type) for shooting down a Heinkel over Germany. They all had been at Cambrai for just over a month, but had got their own Mess (a farmhouse which the Prince of Bavaria had lived in during the last war) & their Flight was very well finished and decorated—the mural in the Mess illustrated a battle between angels and demons, while the hut had an especially modern design, both done by one of their own men. The Flight

(87)   also had a bar in one corner, in addition to various playthings, one depicting a man baisant san femms [baisant sa femme, having sexual intercourse with his wife].

On the 27th Will Gore, Peter Dixon & Peter Parrott pushed off to St Inglevert in the Hillman to collect the 'A' Flight machines there and fly them to Abbeville, where they are to carry out with the Lysander Squadron stationed there. This was done successfully and they returned the following Sunday.

Meanwhile the weather had improved to such an extent [that] normal non-operational flying was again permitted and visibility was such that even the intrepid Harry was able to carry out two successive X-countries without disappearing. Other members of the Flight indulged in the practice known as hagging; WFB was a particular sinner and claimed fourteen hours in four days, a sharp contrast to the total of twenty-five minutes from the month of February; equally

(88)   typical was the day on which our Flight completed 36 hours, more than the total for the Squadron for the previous month. The record was put up on the occasion of an exercise where we were supposed to be defending convoys passing along the Douai–Arras–Bapaume area against low-flying bomber attacks—actually […] the only machine we were able to chase was a Blenheim, which persisted in circling round Arras, even long after it had been shot down. Another enemy was a D.H. on which both sections delivered a No. 1 attack, but apart from the fact that one was flying, it was an unsatisfactory day.

On March a complete fracture of about 1/16 width was found in a longeron of machine 'G', which was really only just back from a long visit to Douai where it had had a new engine fitted. So it was taxied gingerly across to the workshops, and

(89)   Will Gore praised Heaven he had not attempted aerobatics in it, when he had it up a few days ago.

A useful acquisition to the Flight was the Magister and during these days it was flying practically from dawn to dusk. A dawn patrol was also indulged in most mornings, for it was felt that then, if ever, the Hun could be found.

And on March 9th & 10th further command exercises were carried out in which the Hurricanes and us tried to defend a convoy moving South against low-flying by supposedly Squadrons of Battles. But we were no more fortunate than we had been a few days previously and attacks were few. A rather illuminating blunder was over the Crecy, via which the bombers were supposed to be entering our zone. The actual place was SS E of Vitry, while the place we guarded was approximately due West. However as

(90)   a result we captured a wild wood pigeon, which was on Will Es machine on landing. It had one wing damaged, so was reported as a

casualty. The CO phoned the news to Ops who got onto sick quarters and shortly afterwards the ambulance with three Flt Lt M.O.s on board, raced up to the aerodrome only to be sadly disillusioned. A cage was built and the bird nursed back to health; a Form 700 was kept and we thought he was fit for a flight test, the door was opened, but old pigeon was apparently quite happy where he was, for he just came out, hopped about, relieved himself like a gentleman, then went back home again.

On March 12th A.O.C. Blount arrived having flown himself over in a Vega Gull; a lot of raspberries were given before he finally took himself off after lunch.

(91)   Next day one of the leading figures in 607 history packed his bag and departed namely THE Adjutant George White. He had been promoted Squadron Leader and was posted to Glisy near Amiens. His going coincided with a number of other important changes. Milne Irving took over his duties as adjutant, Sq Ldr Harvey went up one place and was to go to 14 Group as SASO: Joe Kayll was to take over command of 615 Squadron, while Francis Blackadder replaced him as O.C. 'A' Flight. With the loss of two pilots, 'A' Flight received a new recruit in Nigel Graeme, who had previously been helping neighbours in 'B' Flight. So the composition of 'A' Flight is now sadly altered from the proud list that heads this diary and reads as follows:

(92)

Flying Officer	W. Francis Blackadder
Flying Officer	Will E. Gore
Flying Officer	George Plinston
Flying Officer	Robert E.W. Pumphrey
Flying Officer	Nigel Graeme
Pilot Officer	H. Peter Dixon
Pilot Officer	Anthony D. Forster
Pilot Officer	Harry P.J. Radcliffe
Pilot Officer	Peter Parrott

In other words four of the original eight are no longer with us, and what we had long been fearing would be produced through casualties is at last being done by postings and promotions. Our airmen however have suffered little change and in practically all respects are identical to the ones who came out with us, with the addition of the January posting of Sergeant Brown en tete.

(93)   Meanwhile as a result of the damage to machine 'E' excitement was caused on the arrival of a signal detailing one pilot to go and collect a new

machine from Ternhill. A draw was made from among the Flying Officers in 'A' Flight and Bobbie was the fortunate one, who had to back his cap immediately, and who disappeared into the blue for many days. But great excitement arose out of the renowned Hurricane talks: our last lot appears to have gone to the first Canadian Squadron to arrive in England and who was supposed to be coming out to Group or to the Blenheim Flight Squadrons at home. But none were available and heated arguments took place as to which Squadron would re-equip first; 615 were the first named but the second round defiantly went to us and it appeared as certain as anything

(94)   can even be out here, that 607 will be the first to go to Rouen.

On the evening of the 13th, a large party went to the NAAF I show in Arras, where George Formby was the star. Johnnie Sample and W.F.B. when bathing at the Grand Cafe next day encountered the company and J.S. was impressed neither by George nor by his clothes.

During the days that followed Hurricanes were the chief subject of local gossip. It was decided once and for all that 607 would re-equip first, and we learned that four machines were waiting for us at Rouen. Jim Bazin and a small party of men were sent to guard over them until our arrival, which was to take the form of a quick move—but the move was not quick in developing for we were still at Vitry on Good Friday March 22nd when the C. in C. R.A.F. Air Marshal Barrett accompanied by our own

(95)   A.O.C. Blount and met by Group Captain Fullard paid us a maiden visit. On the whole he failed to impress; he gave the parade drawn up outside our Nissen hut his usual talk on V.D. and tried after telling us of the admiration the French had for the R.A.F.; he then proceeded to tell us of what was happening in the World at large, making us feel rather like bushmen in the back of beyond. When the parade had marched off, he shook hands and talked to each pilot. He gave 'B' Flight a quick away, before departing on his tour of inspection, which ended at teatime. One incident in the tour is worthy of record, he asked one of the 615 Glasgow men, 'Who are you?' The answer was unabashed: 'Not so badly, thank you Sir.'

(96)   Sunday, March 24th

At 11.40 Will Gore (Z), Bobbie Pumphrey (G), Nigel Graeme (B) [and] Harry Radcliffe (F) took off to do No. 1 Attacks, Robert being the target machine. Nigel and Harry collided and both span in. Both were killed.

Shortly after the crash two Hillmans set out for St Omer with eight players from 61 Wing to play the French Army at rugger; 607 supplied W.F.B., Forster and Peter Parrott; Forster was Captain. Near Notre Dame de Lorette one of the cars burst a tyre when travelling at 60 M.P.H. but good control by the driver [who] brought it safely to a stop. Group Captain Fullard and Wing Co Harvey passed while the tyre was being changed. At St Omer there were throngs of multitudes winding their way up to the ground, and such was the crowd outside the main entrance that we had to go in

(97)   by the side door and climb a fence: a lengthy search found our changing rooms and at 14.40 we were being photographed off stage along with the French XV, & it was very strong and included 6 Internationals, the rest were mostly professionals (ex 13-a-side) on trial caps. The ground was crowded to capacity.

Before the kick-off both teams were introduced to General Girand Commanding the French Army in the North; the maire handed bouquets to the rival Captains who deposited them on the War Memorial. The game itself was not so important and we felt quite satisfied with a 0-29 (five goals, 1 dropped goal) defeat for quite apart from the question of training and cohesion they were clearly in a different class to us. Wing Co. Maxwell, the not too helpful organiser of the game, was the referee and

(98)   some of his decisions did not please the multitudes, lord grant was among the spectators. After the game both teams foregathered appropriately enough at the Cafe de l'Hermaie, and as expected the French Colonel made a painfully rehearsed speech which our English ***** replied in the normal English manner. Champagne and a garliccy sandwich the fare provided, but the high light of the séance was a speech by the big, bushy black bearded Mayor of St Omer, who it appeared was also the local P.T. king man; he ended his talk off by handing a bronze plaque 'Education physique, efforts bar le minister' to our captain, whose fitness some of us had suspected. Added tone to the statement of the encounter was lent by the score-board, which read France 1— Angleterre 1.

(99)   England we called ourselves, with occasional lapses to RAF and even to Reds. But whatever one thought about the match, which was really a good affair, the Compe entante [coup entrant?] was well served.

Monday, March 25th–Tuesday, March 26th

Will Turner has received the D.F.C. for his part in the raid on Sylt, when the RAF bombed the seaplane base without stop for six hours. Peter Dixon is now on leave, the first of our Officers to begin his No 2. On Tuesday March 26th Harry and Nigel were buried with full military honours at the British Cemetery at Douai: the coffins have been lying in state at the Vitry Mainies [Mairie]; they were escorted on foot as far as the transport yard and again at the other end: all went very smoothly, though there was an unfortunate hiatus in the middle of the sounding of the Last Post which brought us down from the salute and Tony stepped

(100)   forward as the junior Officer in the supporting party to salute. The other five Officers were Will Gore, Jim Bazin, W.F.B., Bobbie Pumphrey and Dudley Craig. Group Captain Fullard and Wing Co Harvey represented 14 Group.

The same evening there was a monumental flap and for a time we feared the day's proceedings might have to be repeated. We were night-flying. All of a sudden the wind veered 180° from South to North and 10/10ths toat swallowed up the ground. Dudley Craig & Nit Whitty were up doing formation practice [when] they were unable to locate the aerodrome and for the next three and a half hours we had a terrible time trying to locate and help them. The formation was soon split and Nit after half an hour's blind flying during which time he had come down to 200ft without seeing the ground had had enough, throttled back, 'searched for his map' and parted company with his machine at

(101)   3,000ft in complete blackness griel gure part eu Frances. He pulled the cord and was surprised how easily the strain was taken; an almighty thud told that his machine had landed before him, a large tall black object floated past him (a chimney) and he made his landfall between two sheds adjoining a pit. He was still doubtful as to whether or not he had avoided Belgium, for the compass was insisted on reading East the whole time, and it did not help when the first men he met turned out to be Italian; however his mind was soon set at rest and by 10.30 we also had heard the good news. But Dudley was still at large and plots were coming in from both sides of the border, twice he was reported by Regional Control to be steering straight for the aerodrome, and we let off a continuous stream of Very Lights in addition to setting fire to tins of petrol and the usual flare path & flood light equipment. But at 11.30 he was reported

(102)   over Peronne and we knew the climax was approaching, as he must be very near the end of his petrol, having taken off at 21.00 hours. Apparently all of this time he had been steering various compass courses: he had found the revolving balissage at Derain and three times had steered 288° for the aerodrome, but the cloud had driven him lower and lower until he was forced to turn back: finally he set a course for Peronne and sure enough hit some lights which he thought must be it: from there he steered for the A.C. aerodrome and found what he thought was it, and saw the long straight Amiens–St Quentin road. He was now on his gravity tank: he put his head into the cockpit to release a flare and had rather a tussle, during which time he must have drifted away from the aerodrome; No. 1 flare just drifted off. No. 2 was alright, it lit up a ploughed field, so he decided now or never: he motored in purposing

(103)   to touch down by the flare, fortunately realised in time the flare was lying in a deeply sunken road, so pulled over and felt his way onto the ground: one bump, two bumps, forward then slowly the tail came over and he was on his back.

Wednesday, March 27th–Monday, April 8th

The Squadron's run of misfortune continued when Will Gore in 'R' had his engine seize up completely, fortunately he was at a height of 25,000 ft and even though over Bethune was able to forceland comfortably on our own aerodrome. And Sample of all pilots applied the brakes on our latest toy—a split new Master which Bow-Wow Bowen had ferried over from Angleterre—and she was on her nose. Fortunately most of us had in about half an hour each on her; so should now be able to go straight onto Hurricanes when they eventually turn up. Dudley Craig

(104)   relieved Bazin as guardian of the sacred four that were waiting at Rouen. And then we learned that Rouen was off and that we would re-equip at Vitry—a sad disappointment—for Rouen promised fun with its fresh untouched hunting grounds. On April 6th we came a step nearer our goal when Bazin, Young (615) George Plinston, Peter Parrott and a new pilot just posted to 'A' Flight from 87 Sq, a West Indian called Jay, went by Comma to Rouen and flew them back. But were we allowed to fly them? Not on your life. Group laid down that they were not to be touched until another four had arrived—and so we go on operating in these bloody little biplanes with small hope of opening our French count. With the shortage of pilots and machines a new system of keeping watch has been introduced; our section is at readiness from 5.30 am

(105)   until released (generally about 19.30), one section is at 30 minutes 'B'—both these sections can sleep in of the morning. Though are liable to be brought forward to 5 minutes, at any time.

On April 6th Winston Churchill accompanied by the C. in C. RAF paid 615 another visit but stopped no longer than he had on the first occasion. And once again he found that most of his Squadron was on detachment to St Inglevert; but Squadron Leader Joe was there to receive. He appeared to be going down very well with his new companions.

Meanwhile W.F.B. had become an Acting Flight Lieutenant without pay, an honourable rank and pleasing to vanity. He and Montie Thompson visited

(106)   George White at No. 1 R.S. unit and found him struggling with even more work that he had had to face at snooker.

And here is Song we meet in practically every French Mess [...]

(107)   Early in April the famous English wing three-quarter crashed when landing and was killed. He was one of 615, and was just past finishing off his training before coming out to join us in France.

On the political arena it was clear another crisis was approaching and on April 8th we deliberately ignored Norway's neutrality and laid mines along the coast, thus intercepting the Narvik on route to Germany. This was the first of the week's momentous happenings, from the next day i.e.:

(108)   Tuesday, April 9th–Wednesday, April 24th

Hitler invaded Denmark and overcame the country within the space of a few hours, while he also attacked Norway and by the end of the day Oslo, Bergen and Narvik were in German hands. Our Navy and Air Force immediately got busy, and several fierce engagements took place.

The Squadron was not left unaffected and after summons had indicated our probable destination, on the afternoon of Thursday, April 11th, we quietly slipped away to the West and half an hour later landed at Abbeville, where we took over from 26 (A.C.) Squadron, who had been moved to Dieppe. Will Gore had gone on ahead in the Comma and was there to witness the Squadron's arrival in the following manner. CO, Jay line abreast 'A' Flight in echelon and 'B' in Vic.

(109)   put our machines to bed, then followed a rough road right into the heart of a wood some three miles away where there were crowds of Nissen huts for our men and a Chateau for us; hosts of daffodils, violets and

wood. Grand and altogether different from the dreary flatness of Vitry. Our host was an imposing affair and there was room for all of us; we dined off bubbly Champagne and beer and like and dined well.

The next day was visitors' day and included Wing Co Eccles now established with the Wing in Abbeville itself, Group Capt Fullard and later A.O.C. Blount flew himself over and Milne Irving distinguished himself by crossing swords with General Girand when commanding a convoy which was touring Arras.

On the 13th there was an amusing episode between Bobbie Pumphrey

(110)   and his Flight Commander; contrary to his expectations, W.F.B. called him at 5 am and said time to get up. However he regarded this as a nonsense and went to sleep again. A quarter of an hour later he was called again; this time he protested with some heat; 'I wish you wouldn't keep waking me up: I'm trying to get to sleep!' And so to readiness.

The Naval battles off the coast of Norway appear to have ended in our favour & troops have been landed & Narvik is in British hands; the RAF have been sending constant formations of bombers to deal with the aerodromes at Stavanger, Trondheim & Oslo, so a new flap [was] developed lest the Hun took retaliatory measures against Allied bases. We were brought onto Alert No 3 which meant things were getting pretty serious and we prepared to move into Belgium.

(111)   In the middle of it all our oft-repeated prayer received its fulfilment, when on Sunday April 14th ten Hurricanes circled the aerodrome and landed. Squadron Leader Dewar of 87 Squadron led the party and pleased us with a very decent gesture—three bottles of champagne, out of which he drank to our health.

The following evening the CO and the two Flight Commanders did their No. 1 in France and on the 16th we really got cracking and put in 30 hours' flying. The good work was favoured by grand weather and by evening on the 17th most of us had got onto formation and fighter attacks & were quite at home on them. Cheering news was received at lunchtime when we heard we were excused operational flying, with the exception of the section that is being kept at Vitry.

(112)   Our new surroundings were living up to our first expectations and both chaps and men were well pleased. Particularly satisfying was our Mess, where we found to our surprise that ration meat was not only edible but if cooked properly, and not stewed, very good: in fact we stood amazed at all that could be got out of rations and vexed we had been had at the Wing Mess. Bobbie Pumphrey was hard at work with all this, and at

one time appeared to be running the camp. Even camp beds after their first night or two became quite comfortable and generally we were so shagged by the end of the day that sans doubt we would have slept anywhere. Bière blonde and bière brune du Coq hardi proved very much to our taste and altogether tempers were sweeter than they had been for many a day. Even cleanliness was possible

(113)   and deep hot water was waiting for us at the Hotel de la Tete du Beuf in Abbeville.

On the evening of April 18th we had free entertainment from the Orderly Officer, John Hawkes, ably abetted by Doc David, Dudley inter alia. John was drunkenly sorrowful for a junior of his in LNER had been promoted to the rank of captain; the latter two were full of sympathy and made the cause their common affair. A stuffed wild boar from the forest of Crecy was fortified with a peeled banana as a penis and two onions for high balls while blobs of Brylcream were dabbed on the floor and he was christened BOLLAND and placed in John's room: and he was delighted. As an interlude John gave us admirable repertoires on the phone to the R.T.O. at Amiens, and

(114)   when the phone bell rang once again, he picked it up & said 'Me again'—but this time it was 61 Wing from their comfortable house in Abbeville.

On the 22nd we closed down early and both the Comma and the Hillman took bodies into Le Touquet where there was dispersal. Jim & Francis were seen to admire Kabul, an Afghan wolfhound, and Scottie, an Aberdeen terrier, which were romping about the sands and whose mistresses were comely to look upon. Jay and others laid hard a baby electrics and drove the streets in fine fettle. There was a reassembly at Harry's bar and we all fed at the Hotel du Centre, a further dispersal took place and on this occasion there was no reunion for these bodies, to witt those of Jim, Francis and Milne [who] were inadvertently left behind. These bodies were not best pleased and after an uneventful night at the Centre turned up the following morning at the aerodrome in a taxi and still very heated.

[Written up the side:] (On the 21st, when at Vitry jay [Trevor Jay] was directed to a Hun by APO Fine [in] a Do 17 at 22,000ft, he got in a burst at 500 yds, as it flashed past in a dive.)

(115)   The next day Francis, Bobbie and Ashton flew their Hurricanes across to Vitry and in the evening, one week after their pilot's first solo.

Red Section (W.F.B., R.E.W.P., A.D.F) took off on the first Squadron Hurricane patrol and searched the skies 28,000ft above Seclin & Douai for a Hun that did not appear.

On the 24th the above echelon of the Squadron returned to Vitry headed by John Hawkes and Hine the French interpreter attached to us.

Thursday, April 25th–Friday, May 10th

The remainder of the Squadron followed fast and the next fortnight we were busy completing our training and doing odd patrols. I went on leave so missed what fun there was. [pages no longer carry numbers]

(118)   Friday, May 10th–Monday, May 20th

In the early hours of Friday the Hun crossed the frontiers of Holland, Belgium and Luxembourg. The Squadron were unaware of this for some time and still respected these countries' neutrality when they ran into hordes of bombers which fled across what was to us a Border. However heavy toll was affected and in that first day over 20 machines must have been shot down; I was meanwhile returning to the unit, excitement in London town was intense when the news of the various violations leaked there & ARP precautions were once more practiced. Dover was full of minions. But one thing was certain: the BEF had moved into Belgium. Not knowing where we would find 607 Milne

(119)   Irving laid in an ample supply of chocolate & brandy wine as our rations. The crossing was quiet but Boulogne was on edge; German machines had circled round the town at 600ft earlier on and bombed mainly aerodromes: we had six hours there & during that time five separate air raid alarms sounded. And when it was dark our train sneaked away and eventually we reached Arras. No sooner did we get out than the drone of a Boch machine could be heard: we spent the night at the commerce & took the early train on to Vitry where very much to our surprise we found the rest of the Squadron. The first person I saw was Will Gore & he

(120)   passed on the thrilling news of the yesterday's battle; he himself had got four in the one day, and according to his report it was all money for jam. But Johnnie Sample had not been so fortunate and had bailed out after downing his man; his ankle was badly sprained on landing. One of the new men in our Flight, Weatherill, was missing, but 36 hours

later he turned up with 'How are you, folks.' Total for the day about 30 hours.

And so to battle. The best way of telling the story of these ten days is to give each individual's history. First of all mine, cos that is norm best, tho' it is hazy af [after] another ops.

(121)   My first job was soon after breakfast on the 11th when I led a Flight of six to patrol West of Brussels along the line Grammont–Lassines–Ath: the weather was filthy at our end but cleared as we sped North; we were protecting the BEF as they moved up East and there was not interference during our hour on patrol.

In the afternoon we came back on the same job though this time the line was further East, namely Ninov, Enghien and Soignies; we had only carried out one run when Jim Bazin, who was leading one section waggled his wings and set off after a solitary machine flying East; we followed and eventually took the lead; machine turned out to be a Heinkel and after several attacks by us it went down in smoke and burst into flames on hitting the ground. We circled round then Peter Dixon set off further East: I followed and soon saw a dozen

(122)   machines; a few minutes later we spotted another dozen bombers converging on the first group and behind them two and one; we left the groups and eventually I got in an attack under heavy canon fire on the Dornier; I broke off and was climbing to renew the attack when I saw a group of single engines arriving; thinking they were French or British I climbed up to meet them, but they were Messerschmidt 109s in force so I had to run; at ground level over German territory with plunge pulled until eventually when well into my gravity tank and with oil streaming down my left wing I decided the time had come to land. I found a field and landed with room to spare. But no sooner landed than I saw a bomber overhead, so having convinced some Belgian soldiers I was on their side, I tarried quickly to one hedge & got the machine

(123)   quickly camouflaged with branches and earth clods: I then found I was near Hannut and that the Hun was not far away; I had a hole in my oil tank, little oil remained. However after 5 hours coping with the Belgians and fighting my way thro' streams of refugees I was refuelled with a sort of aviation spirit and mobilised; an exciting take-off as I forgot to go into fine pitch & I scraped past some trees before flying South to hit the Meuse near Huy; no sooner here than 2 Huns set on me & I had to fly below the river banks and corner like a motoracer skimmed the roofs of Namur & it was not until I had passed Charleroi that I dared pull up; and another shock was

in store for a badly shaken pilot, because a machine suddenly bobbed up on my right—fortunately a Morane; landed with fading light to

(124) the surprise and relief of everybody. But Peter was missing and it was only 2 days later that he turned up; after giving up the chase he had circled a railway station to find it was Achen, [Aachen] so he flew and he flew until eventually he landed near Tirlemont. While [he was] searching for juice, the Hun came and bombed his machine, so he had to foot it to Brussels & so via the Air Attaché back to Vitry.

The same day Will Gore was shot down in flames but managed to jump, though received severe shock and after some days in hospital was sent back to England. And friend Jay got a hole in his leg and off he went too.

On the 12th I was leading a Flight of 607, which joined up with other Flights from 615, 85 & 87 Squadrons over Sedan for an offensive patrol

(125) we flew East over Maastricht and then turned South; set on by Me 109s and He 112s; after a short battle I escaped with a steep climbing turn to the right, and after flying over forest after forest landed in a field just south of St Quentin: had sufficient petrol to fly home after satisfying the French authorities as to my identity.

On the 13th a Squadron of 607 & 615 undertook another offensive patrol and SE of Louvain ran into a crowd of dive bombers attacking our troops. I appeared to shoot down three, one in flames & two damaged; all Henschel 123s before having to beat a strategic withdrawal from a He 112; on the way back went through some telephone wires without

(126) misfortune, but my aircraft was riddled with holes from the Henschels' quarter attacks and both compasses had been pierced.

That afternoon both the CO & Montie Thompson failed to return.

The next day on a similar patrol got among some Me 109s with my sights U/S owing to the rheostat being turned off, so I was glad to get away; over Valenciennes saw AA fire and found nine He 111s; delivered a quarter attack and tried to spray them with bullets before diving away home; heavy fire on me. In the evening we went to Douai & my undercarriage collapsed after a bad landing—I went on my nose without injury to myself but lovely new

(127) rotol was a wreck.

The next filthy job I remember was providing an escort for Blenheims that were carrying out photographic reconnaissance East of Brussels; when that was complete we patrolled near Hal for a time before returning home without combat.

On the 17th I led a Squadron on an offensive patrol in the area East of Le Cateau; we had no sooner arrived than we spotted some Heinkels and a Do 17; seven of the former and the latter were shot down; I was fired at by a Hurricane with British markings and it also chased Stewart for about 10 mins. The Hun is also using a Lysander with our markings. In the evening I carried out a reconnaissance of the Cambrai–Le Cateau road. Earlier on the usual Hun reconnaissance machine had been heard over Vitry: suddenly to

(128)   our horror he dived down, dropped bombs near the railway line then proceeded to machine-gun & bomb the oil refinery just past —: Flights took off after him as he circled our base at 100 ft and he did not live long, but the oil was alight & it was days before the fires could be put out.

But May 18th was to be der Tag: it started well; Stewart & I were on a security patrol of base when we were told over the R/T of a bandit SE of Vitry; spotted it immediately, took up position, it dived to ground level & used full evasion tactics; I got in my rounds and knocked out the rear gunner; then Stewart took over & both disappeared. I started off home, when my engine

(129)   seized, oil pressure at zero, and I was at 600 ft [and] had to forceland with legs up in the nearest field; easily ejected & only a slight bump on the forehead; some miners helped me remove the 8 Browning guns, compass, Sperry panel and clock, while a crippled schoolmaster lent me his car; we were West of Valenciennes and had a hard ride back through streams of refugees. The Hun was advancing rapidly towards St Quentin and Cambrai.

Shortly after getting back S/Ldr Jackson told me I had been selected on account of my local knowledge to lead four Squadrons of fighters and four Squadrons of bombers on a raid East of Cateau. Hardly had the machines taken off than a dozen Me 109s dived down and were among us before we knew

(130)   they were there; it was slaughter and five went down: I took off into it and was very frightened, climbed high thro' cloud & then got among them; after that led some bombers to their objectives; on landing broke down. But 5 minutes later the Heavens were rent with gunfire and a tremendous battle was staged between our Hurricanes and the Me 110s: Mars was indeed angry.

A quiet patrol then the third battle of Vitry began; we saw some Do⁵ flying low near Arras, so we took off, AA fire high up over Aras & saw 9/12 enemy aircraft; thought they were Do 17s but they were Me 110s and while we were engaged with them the Do⁵ flew low over our aerodrome [and]

(131)   dropped incendiary bombs and continued to do so all along the Douai road. I landed for safety at Douai aerodrome. After some difficulty got started & returned to Vitry to find 'B' Flight & workshops had lost several machines & new Squadrons on the North side lost about 6 or 7. It was decided to move & off we went as soon as we could to Norrent Fontes; all old crocks were destroyed [and] we landed at our new base in the gloaming and with the assistance of two helpful French Armée de L'Air [who] found food and billets of a sort. The convoy arrived about 3 am and we were well rid of Vitry as both

(132)   the aerodrome and the village itself was heavily bombed during the night.

On the evening of the 19th Jim Bazin and I volunteered for the reconnaissance to be carried out of the German areas East of Brussels: we flew over Ypres, Ploegsteert and just as we separated Jim was receiving a baptism of fire from our own Bofors; this increased, so finally he had to give up and return to base; I arrived at my job at 100 ft and 230 MPH and reported on German mechanised column seen. No AA fire nor enemy fighters encountered but it was not a pleasant job.

The next day Jim and I were part of the five war-weary pilots

(133)   flown home to Hendon from Merville in a Douglas. At Merville we found our Acklington III friend in charge, W. Co Broadhurst DFC AFC.

Earlier in the week I had done 500 MPH in a dive.

Just before we left, good old Stoo-art [Stewart] turned up, as shaken as ever a man I've seen; he chased after the Do that got me and shot it down, then just as he was about to return home, he saw another, so chased it for some time & got in an attack; he decided it was time to return, as his petrol was running low, and soon he found an aerodrome, but as he was circling to reconnoitre the bomb holes he was met by a

(134)   fusillade of shots & he saw the Hun was in occupation—Maubeuge; he continued his flight until his petrol was exhausted then landed with u/c up in a field, which was 5 miles our side of the lines near Rheims; he was taken prisoner by the French and not released until British RAF appeared; while on their aerodrome the place was bombed to hell, so he went to another one further South; this too was being evacuated and just as he was taking off as passenger in a Blenheim, the machine next him was blown up by a bomb, but they reached Glisy safely & George

(135)   White found him abed & next he got one of the new rotol Hurricanes and shot down a Junkers 88 that was bombing the aerodrome;

he landed to re-arm but no sooner had he done so than ten Me 110s dived out of the sky and machine-gunned the place—to him the next most terrifying of all his experiences as bullets seemed to be going through his hair, but evidently, they went & he was alive & able to fly, another total bad to us at Norrent Fortes.

Jim Bazin was also missing

(136)   for a long time: he forcelanded near Sedan after having tried without success to bale out from the left hand side; he was shot at, so escaped into a wood and through a field of corn to a road where he found a French motor cyclist. He was taken to their general & made welcome, but they were in retreat—so back he went to set fire to his machine, but a hail of bullets from the Hun line made him decide it was better to leave things as they were. He accompanied general, who was getting all his men back across the canal & then [to] blow up the

(137)   bridge; made in a stand; and eventually got a conveyance home.

The whole show was like the film Dawn Patrol but it was given bitter reality.

Fidler, the Armaments Officer ex Group took over command of the Squadron on the 17th as Johnnie Sample was likely to be u/s for some time: on the evening of the next day he put up a hell of a show by flying a Hurricane from Vitry & landing at night at Seclin. His total of hours on this type was under five. The next day when leading an offensive patrol over Dinant, he failed to return and was last seen heavily engaged by five Me 109s.

On the 20th Robert Pumphrey went missing after a ground-strafing job along the Bapaume / Arras road. He was seen to bale out, but it was many weeks before.

(138)   Smoke from Oil wells at Dunkirk drifting down Channel seen on our training flights.

(139)   We heard that [Robert Pumphrey] like Will Turner was a prisoner of war—enlightenment please. This was actually 607's last job in France.

In the early afternoon the order for instant withdrawal was received, those who could get machines flew back across the Channel; the rest made their way as best they could to the coast & to England. Many of them had incredible adventures and amazing experiences, but not a single man was lost. Heavy bombing of Boulogne & Abbeville took place while they were there. At Boulogne red tape managed to survive, for it was necessary to obtain a ticket from Officer 'A' and hand it to Officer 'B' before permission to proceed on board ship was granted.

In the days that followed the Squadron slowly reassembled at Croydon; James Vick arrived fresh from Ops Room at Tangmere and was a welcome new CO

(140)   but it meant that Johnnie Sample had to go and we were all very pleased when we heard he had gone to 504, they had been with us at Norrent Fortes and had received a terrible hammering; they were now reforming at Wick.

Less palatable movements followed and in two days we lost all those officers who had come to us in the stress of the battle and also George Plinston, Ian Stewart & Dini; The BEF's retreat to Dunkirk was at full, and our fighter Squadrons was losing heavily each day.

We had already been greatly incensed to hear that all five of the war wearies had been posted away to other Squadrons within 48 hours of their arrival home. Peter Dixon & Peter Parrott with Scratchy Ashton went to Tangmere, John Humpherson

(141)   to Debden and Tony Forster to North Weald. Not many days elapsed before Peter Dixon was posted missing while operating over Dunkirk, while Dini was killed in a flying accident.

In fact all that remained of the old No. 607 Squadron at Croydon was:

'A' Flight	'B' Flight
W.F. B.	Jim Bazin
Milne Irving	Dudley Craig
	Nit Whitty
	Chatty Bowen

& John Hawkes as Intelligence Officer—David Smith as M.O.—while Taylor who had come to us in times of stress out there as Squadron Adjutant, also remained.

However Will Gore was soon to make his escape from the 'lameless' and

(142)   nurses at Torquay and rejoin 'A' Flight, but Jay [up]on his wound healing preferred to rejoin his old unit 85 Sq at Church Fenton.

'A' Flight pilots were:

Lance Smith	—	Missing, 13 May '40
Francis Blackadder	—	Sain et Sauf
Will Gore	—	In hospital, 12 May '40
Robert Pumphrey	—	Missing, 20 May '40, PoW

Peter Dixon	—	Missing, 27 May '40
D.T. Jay	—	In hospital, 12 May '40
Fidler	—	Missing, 19 May '40
Cuthbert	—	Missing, 12 May '40
Weatherill	—	Missing, 18 May '40
Peter Parrott	—	Posted after sick leave
Tony Forster	—	Posted after sick leave
Ian Stewart	—	Posted from Croydon
George Plinston	—	Posted from Croydon
Demetriadi	—	Posted from Croydon
Dini	—	Posted later killed
Sgt Ralls	—	Posted
Russell	—	Missing
Milne Irving	—	Sain et Sauf

(143)   Milne had perhaps been leading the most adventurous life during the Blitz, as he and one other Gladiator—in every sense of the word—had been defending our aerodromes at Peronne, Poix etc. He did not shoot any of his Hun offenders down, but did frighten several and himself perhaps even more.

The official cap of the Squadron from these memorable ten days was registered as seventy-three, believed a record—while it is probable, [the official cap] actually may have been twice that number.

After the battle, Croydon, seemed quiet and the Squadron or those that remained were not best pleased when they learned from Daddy Probyn that it was to become a training establishment for the next weeks and it required

(144)   the announcement of the award of the DFC to will Gore and of the DSO & DFC to Joe Kayll to make our head lift. Joe's Squadron had had a pretty lousy time of it and had lost heavily with their Auxiliary officers; Joe had himself put up a hell of a show and had been the life & soul of 615; they were now de retour to Kenley, their home station, but unlike us had the more noble [task] of trying to protect the BEF at Dunkirk.

On June 4th further awards were made & this time W.F.B. featured with a D.S.O. and Johnnie Sample got a DFC. And the same day this chapter of the Squadrons history came to an end where it began—at Usworth, for at 13.30 hours we took off from

(145)   Croydon in separate sections of three, and passing over Oxford, Nottingham, York, once again saw Penshaw monument before us, but a new Usworth—two concrete runways and a perimeter track covering a much enlarged aerodrome.

We landed & two very welcome old faces were at the dispersal point waiting for us—Fanny Adams & Dob Wardale.

607 had returned home.

(146)   Peter Dixon at La Heritriere in Lille in 1940, having dined exceedingly well and making a suitable exit, but his path is baulked by gentlemen in khaki. 'I wish these bloody second lieuts would get out of my way'—stumble and headlong plunge into the tummy of the second lieut—who was unfortunately a Major General.

NB Individual Pilots Stories of those days.

(151)   3. IX. 39
Airmen

Flight Sergeant Barrett Atkinson	Fitter
Sergeant Fort	Fitter II
Corporal Parker	Fitter II
Corporal Gibson	Metal rigger

Gladiator		Rigger	Fitter
B 8030		Blackclock	Shotton
D 7983		Taylor	Darke
E 6147	(Reserve)	Blackclock	Shotton
F 8000		Green	Dowley
G 7989	(Reserve)	Fowler	Dixon
H 7988		Stewart	Reay
R 7898		Fowler	Dixon
W 7997		Frazer	Thompson
Z In place of W			

Wireless Operator	Ac Bell
Electrician	Ac Elliot
ACH	Crow
	Hall
	Gallantry

Armourers	Cpl MacDonald
	Moore
	Wright
	Johnston

Mascot	Barney

(152)   Peter along with Tony Forster & eight or ten others had been coming home from Vitry aerodrome when No. 607 Squadron had been stated as on rest. Often criticised at the beginning of flying & fighting since the beginning of the Blitz Krieg.

Friday, 10th May 1940

He [Peter] said they had no idea they were being sent homeward that day, in fact he had been patrolling the area of Brussels that morning at 3 am from where he came in, he was told by G to get his things quickly together and get into the plane.

He only brought things that would go in his pack or all would fall into the German's hands a few days later. The squadron itself had to leave Vitry aerodrome by this Monday, May 22nd (The Germans having reached there). On Saturday Peter & Francis Blackadder were patrolling looking for German planes; they damaged one, which fell burning into the ground; he was duly cremated.

They then saw two enemies & went after them closing them in & lots of clouds. In the chase Peter lost sight of Blackadder, then it was learnt afterwards [that he] had run out of petrol, but finally had managed to get hold of some

(153)   and set back to his aircraft after a few hours. Peter continued chasing the enemy plane in and out of clouds hoping it was Belgium & France, he came down low to see if he could make out Qrane Station and he was greeted with a hail of A.A. shells so climbed up as quickly as he could and flew west. Petrol by then was running very low, he looked about for somewhere to descend; he then saw below him a shell battered aerodrome with one small plane that looked fairly possible & managed to land his plane safely. (As he said, striding up driving in the way the old C13 is driven by two families) he taxied in between the craters to the other side of the aerodrome where he saw a main road (there was a transport convoy of passing Belgian troops and so he waited for it to stop). As Peter expressed it, he sat on a bank and 'sulked'. Finally a young Belgian officer came up and asked him who he was and what was his nationality. Peter said English & pointed to his plane, he had already disposed of his parachute as it was too risky to keep it due to the state of tension in Belgium and due to the use of German parachute troops in the Belgian offensive. The Belgian officer took him to his Colonel who then questioned him.

(154)   He [the Belgian Colonel] insisted he must be a German as his French was too good to pass as an Englishman! Peter denied this and finally convinced the Colonel when he pulled some of my letters out of his pocket and said, 'Here are some of my letters sent to me, you can see that they are in English.' The Belgian Colonel finally sent him off with 4 young officers to hunt for petrol. They scoured the countryside several times having to leave the car & dive into a ditch as German planes flew over machine-gunning refugees on the road. They found some lorry petrol at last & got it back to the aerodrome only to find that the Germans had been there & the Hurricane was completely out of action. He decided to get back to Brussels & travelled part of the way with refugees & partly with a Belgian man with whom he had a hair raising drive, the man relying critically on his horn which he blew wildly all the time to clear a way through the masses of relentless population—a terrifying experience, Peter said.

Later he hailed a passing lorry piled with Belgian airmen going back to Brussels (their aerodrome having been bombed & obliterated). Peter had a talk with them

(155)   for a time till he decided they were travelling [...] to Brussels. So he left them, later a British officer came along & and after some talk offered Peter a lift to Brussels in his car. When they arrived Peter was given a room in the half of a large Chateau belonging to the Duc de Guise & lent by him to the RAF. He said that his room was all fancy with tapestries. It was very late and he was glad of a few hours sleep. Next morning the Wing Co took Peter to the Belgian HQ & told him to stay and answer questions & impress the Belgians with the excellent work being done by the RAF. Little news had come to them & there was much depression. Peter said it was a great strain on his French but he did his best. He was told he had just missed the King of the Belgians who had just left a few minutes before after being introduced to Sir Roger Keys who had asked him many questions & had taken him to see the British ambassador Sir Lancelot Hiplant. Peter was much taken with his size and his wide delivery of oaths (Gods teeth etc) giving his thanks to 607 & repeated Peter was safe and sound and would shortly rejoin his unit which he did later that day.

Written Sunday May 12th. Peter.

5

Post France

As mentioned in the previous chapter, Blackadder was awarded the DSO on 4 June 1940, in time for his return to Usworth. The citation for the award reads,

> This officer shot down three enemy aircraft and led his patrols with judgement and excellent offensive spirit. In particular he carried out singly several extremely important reconnaissances of bridges and roads at a time when other means of obtaining news were not effective. His reports were very valuable to the Army.

Once back at Usworth, the squadron wasted no time getting on with its training duties. Blackadder carried out three flights on 6 June, all in P2874 AF-F, and all were formation flights. However, for Blackadder a change to the routine began on 8 June. On this day and for the next few days, Blackadder's duties were to accompany Lord Trenchard around 13 Fighter Group on his morale boosting visits. The flights were carried out in a DH 86, N6246, piloted by Fg Off. Jeffries. The tour began at Church Fenton and Kirton-in-Lindsey, continuing on to Thornaby and Acklington on 9 June. On the 10 June, the tour continued to Woolsington, Turnhouse (now Newcastle airport), Leuchars and Drem. From this point onwards, Blackadder's duties were complete and he was to make his return to Usworth flying himself in a Master.

Over the next few days Blackadder flew a variety of Hurricanes as he got down to the more routine business of training. Mostly these were formation flights, later intermixed with cross-country flights, mainly to Acklington, and a few test flights for 'pip-squeak' (R/T tests) and various homing duties. From 20 June, he began check-out flights with some of the new pilots that were joining the squadron. He began with Sgt Glover in the passenger on circuits and landings in the Magister. He also carried out check-out flights, in the Magister or Master, with Sgt's Hewitt and Burnell-Phillips, pilots newly posted from the OTU.[1]

Also making a return to the squadron was Harry Welford. Welford states that he was given a choice of Flights to join; he picked 'A' Flight because he knew Blackadder well, whom he referred to as a 'Dutch Uncle'. However, things did not go well. Welford had joined as 'operational', but now found he had to do a further month's training: this he found tedious, since he had done the work already at OTU, and two of his friends—John Lenahan and Stuart Parnall—were on 'B' Flight, so socialising was not too good. Welford then found that Blackadder's paternalism exceedingly seeped into squadron discipline, which did not suit. One night, Welford crashed a car into a road block in Gateshead: called to see Blackadder the following morning, he was read the riot act, and Blackadder told him that he drank too much, was wasting time, and was generally 'playing silly buggers'. Blackadder voiced the opinion that he would be better off in 'B' Flight with his friends—Welford, jumped at the chance, and soon departed for 'B' Flight.[2]

Harry Welford.

The rest of June saw Blackadder back into the routine of cross-country flights combined with instrument and night flying exercises, as well as fighter tactics. Most of these flights were carried out in Hurricane P3667. Throughout July, air activity in the south was beginning to heat up; back at Usworth, it was a simple case of increased concentration on fighter tactics in training. Exercises carried out by the pilots included Attack No. 3 and air interceptions intermixed with quick getaways and formation flights.

In early June, another of the 'original' hands returned to the squadron. Will Gore, after suffering from burns from being shot down in France, had spent time in a Torquay hospital. After a period of home leave, Gore was posted back to No. 607 Squadron, and arrived back at Usworth on 22 June. 'Gore was soon to make his escape from the 'lameless' and nurses at Torquay and rejoin 'A' Flight,' entered Blackadder into his diary. Will Gore's name is also in the list of pilots in 'A' Flight of No. 607 Squadron entered in Blackadder's diary at this time. Gore is thought to have been flying with No. 54 Squadron in July and August, because No. 607 Squadron was on detachment at Catterick during this period, and No. 54 Squadron was also based there. Based on this coincidence alone, Gore is supposed to have been active as part of No. 54. As recently as 2012, a plaque was placed in the Ian Ramsey School at Stockton proclaiming that Will Gore, of Nos 607 and 54 Squadrons, was once a pupil there. From such things are myths born.

William Ernest Gore.

On 22 July, Blackadder flew 'F' on an RIT test, and later that same day, No. 607 Squadron was passed as operational, although by day only. For the rest of the month, Blackadder noted that he carried out the usual formula of cross-country flights and night flying, mostly in Hurricane 'G'. He also partook in a low-flying bombing raid—the target was unspecified, but was more than likely one of the ranges. His total count for night flying for the month was four-and-a-half hours.

As August began, routine remained similar: various cross-country flights, mixed with patrols. One flight that was out of the ordinary came on 5 August. Blackadder notes that he made a local flight in a Spitfire, the only identification of which was the individual aircraft code letter 'J' (the unit it belonged to was not revealed). During this period, flights rotated on detachment to Catterick: this cut down patrol time because most patrols went over convoys, more often than not in the area off the north Yorkshire coast, Scarborough, and Whitby. The cover of convoy 'Arena' was one such patrol, some 30 miles south-east of Scarborough on 7 August. Two days later, Blackadder was in a formation that attacked a He 111 off Sunderland, which he then recorded was shot down by an aircraft of No. 79 Squadron.

So far, so quiet—but all was to change dramatically on the afternoon of 15 August. Blackadder had been carrying out aerobatics in P2874 'F' when *Luftflotte V* struck at all fronts of Britain's defences simultaneously. *Luftflotte V* launched an attack from Stavanger, Norway, on Driffield, a minor bomber airfield in Yorkshire. The formation was attacked— principally by Nos 72 and 79 Squadrons, with one flight from No. 605 Squadron—and was therefore in some disarray by the time it reached the mouth of the River Tyne. Jim Vick was not flying that day, so it was Blackadder who led the squadron against the enemy formation.

No. 607 Squadron had been brought to readiness almost as soon as the enemy had first been sighted. Harry Welford bemoaned the fact that they sat around the flights for half an hour.[3] Once airborne, no one appeared to know where the enemy was. Blackadder was ordered to go first one way then another before going back to give cover to the airfield at Usworth, wrongly thought to be under attack.[4] Eventually, No. 607 were ordered to the mouth of the Tyne, where they encountered the enemy over Whitley Bay. Many were the claims of seeing aircraft going down; but in reality, few did.

Blackadder's logbook merely records: '607 patrol Seaham 20.000 feet 50 + He111 and Do attacked, 2 uncertain ⅓ certain' and 'Total for 607: 10–8 damaged, some badly'. With the benefit of hindsight, this was considered a highly optimistic score, however. Blackadder was right to point out that many bombers were severely damaged and failed to make it back home;

either crashing into the sea or over land near their base, they were still lost to the Luftwaffe. On a personal front, Blackadder reported that 'F' had received a number of bullet holes in its rear fuselage due to return fire from the enemy force. This observation was written on the rear of a photograph of 'F'. Though later attacked by Spitfires of No. 41 Squadron, the bomber force failed to reach its target—Driffield—and turned for home.

Blackadder did not fly again until 17 August. On this day he carried out tests with the Station Flight, and with the DH constant speed propeller in Hurricane P2680. Otherwise it was once more back to normality, with various attacks and formation flights to the fore, though mainly of the training variety. Blackadder worked his Flight through various scenarios—a move to the south would not be far off. There was still a lot of cross-country back and forth between Usworth and Catterick, and one off-duty moment on 6 September, when on a flight from Usworth, Blackadder flew 'F' on some aerobatics up to 25,000 ft—the peace before the storm. That was it for the day, and Blackadder had the next day off, because the squadron was due to move to the south on the 8th.

Blackadder flew south in Hurricane 'F', from Usworth to Tangmere, on 8 September, making a stop at Bicester. As he left County Durham heading for battle for the second time, he must have wondered—as Harry Welford did—if and when he would ever see it again. The squadron was to take over from a battle-weary No. 43 Squadron at Tangmere, and the airfield alone must have been a bit of a shock to the pilots fresh from the north. Welford's first impressions were as follows:

Hurricane P2874, Blackadder's 'F', at Swoth on 16 August 1940. Note the repeated white 'F'.

We arrived at a completely blitzed aerodrome and were greeted by the remains of 43 Squadron, some on crutches, others with their arms in slings and yet another with his head swathed in bandages.

It was unlikely to be a shock for Blackadder: he had, after all, witnessed worse in France just over two months previously. However, it was soon made clear that the squadron had to be on its toes. It had hardly had time to get the aircraft refuelled when it was scrambled to Shoreham at 15,000 feet, where there was no sign of the enemy, but only AA fire to the east of Brighton.

The following day began quietly, with a patrol over Selsey Bill at 15,000 feet, followed by a sector reconnaissance—all with nothing seen. The final flight of the day was somewhat different. No. 607 Squadron was ordered to the area of Tunbridge Wells, and according to Will Whitty, suffered at the hands of new controllers who were under training: after moving in the wrong direction, the squadron encountered a large number of bombers but failed to see the escorting fighters.[5] Jim Vick was leading the squadron and attacking the bombers.

Blackadder, at the head of Red Section, was some way behind and still in the climb when they were 'bounced' by Me 109s. This was only their

A rare group shot at Tangmere, September 1940: Spyer (third from the left), Blackadder (fourth from the right), and Irving (third from the right).

second day in the south, what happened in the next few seconds can only be described as carnage. Drake and Lenahan went missing—Drake was to remain so until 1972—and Parnall, Spyer, and Landsdell were all shot down; Burnell-Phillips and Stephenson were both injured; and Jim Bazin's Hurricane P3668 was damaged to such an extent that he had to make a forced landing.[6] On their first full day, No. 607 Squadron had lost half its aircraft in one attack. Welford, who did not fly on that patrol, commented, 'We bit back our tears and sorrow'. His feelings no doubt resonated with the whole squadron.

Not all of Blackadder's flights were offensives against the enemy. On 12 September, he records that he flew Hurricane 'UF'—no number or individual aircraft letter recorded—on a ferry flight from Westhampnett to Tangmere. This may have been a replacement aircraft for one of those lost on 9 September, and not a very successful one at that; in Blackadder's own words, 'Ferry 601 dead-beat Hurricane from 213 Squadron'.[7]

On 13 September, Blackadder led a head-on attack against a formation of Ju 88s in the area between Beachey Head and Hastings. After the initial head-on attack he noted that one Ju 88 dropped his undercarriage; but the formation must have recovered quickly, because Blackadder noted that all three Ju 88s made good their escape into the clouds. He must have been reminded of his days over the Channel when, upon chasing them, he ran short of fuel and was forced to make a landing at Shoreham before returning to Tangmere. He recorded a similar scenario on 14 September, when he was leading Red Section: he attacked Ju 88s over Selsey Bill, and they too made their getaway using cloud cover.

15 September saw a turn of events that would later be commemorated as 'Battle of Britain Day'—but it did not begin in too spectacular a style for No. 607 Squadron, or Blackadder. He led Red Section flying Hurricane P4189, in the first patrol of the day. No. 607 Squadron—led by Jim Bazin, according to Blackadder—joined forces with fellow auxiliary squadron No. 602, and they patrolled along a line between Beachy Head and Mayfield at 15,000 feet. Sandy Johnstone, leading No. 602 Squadron, remembers that they patrolled for just short of an hour without encountering anything worthwhile. Blackadder records a flight of an hour and ten minutes and 'Nothing seen'. Such were the frustrations even at the height of the Battle of Britain.

Throughout September, the endless patrols all too often resulted in 'nothing seen'. Blackadder led many such patrols, and was critical of the controllers, for there were occasions when the squadron would arrive at its destination, only to find that the enemy had already departed. On 17 September, Blackadder led Red Section and Jim Bazin Green and Blue Sections in a combined sweep with Nos 602 and 213 Squadrons over the Thames estuary. Red Section, after landing and refuelling, set off to join Bazin's sections, but could not locate the formation, which had been well and truly 'bounced'; both Harry Welford and John Lansdell were shot down, and the latter killed. Sandy Johnstone knew nothing until he saw two of Jim Vick's weavers go down, and Blackadder's logbook states nothing was engaged, making no note of the two fallen pilots: after refuelling, Blackadder's Red Section had not caught up with the others.[8] In his logbook, Jim Bazin sets down no more than that he was 'operational'.[9]

Blackadder made a brief return to the north on 24 September, when he flew Magister 2392 with Flight Sergeant (FS) Anderson in the passenger seat, from Tangmere to Hucknall. The following day, he extended the journey to Catterick, possibly for leave. On 26 September, he made the return flight to Tangmere flying solo. He returned to Tangmere in time to take part in two patrols, and intercepted and attacked a He 111 and an Me 110; he claimed them both, shooting them down near Southampton.

Blackadder flew five patrols on 27 September, two of them along with Nos 213 and 602 Squadrons. The following day, both Will Gore and Milne Irving were posted missing after a patrol over Selsey Bill. Blackadder was not on that patrol, but flew a search pattern of the area looking for the two missing pilots; he makes no mention of their loss in his logbook, only of the search. As two long-standing friends and comrades, he must have felt their loss deeply.

Blackadder flew three sorties on 30 September, two of which were in the company of No. 213 Squadron. After nothing seen in the first two, he carried out an attack on an Me 110 off Chesil Beach, and a Ju 88, Do 17, and Me 109 were also attacked. Of these he recorded two definite, one probable and one damaged; the Me 109 came to 'Nil'.

From 1 to 5 October, Blackadder flew nine patrols, all of them in Hurricane P3929—the aircraft which Harry Welford had been shot down in on 17 September. On 2 October, Blackadder attacked a Ju 88: 'I fired all my ammunition into the Ju 88 without apparent result'. The following day he was on patrol over Swanage when the formation was badly 'bounced' by Me 109s: 'W.F.B., Bazin. Spyer, Evens shot down by Me 109s: all pilots safe'. Blackadder becomes guarded in his logbook comments here. Bazin was leading the squadron, and Blackadder warned him that he thought he saw aircraft to the rear, but Bazin made no reply; PO John Sulman, flying rear-guard, saw the enemy and called out a warning, and the Hurricanes broke all over the sky—the call from Sulman probably saved their lives. Blackadder's luck did not improve that day; flying Anson 9906, he recorded that 'W.F.B. force landed on 'C' aerodrome, glycol'.

Blackadder flew twice in a Magister to an unspecified destination on 7 October, and returned to flying patrols on 9 October, when he made one

Blackadder riggers FS Barret-Aitken and Sgt Fort at Tangmere.

flight but made no comment on it at all in his logbook. His next two flights were in 'F' on 10 October, the first of which was a patrol in which 'Many fighters seen, presumed friendly'; the second flight was northwards, for No. 607 Squadron departed Tangmere for Catterick. Blackadder did not fly again until 13 October, on which day he flew from Catterick to Turnhouse in Hurricane V7223. Once again, No. 607 Squadron had returned home from battle.

Throughout October, Blackadder's time was divided between Turnhouse and Drem, where the squadron still maintained detachments. On 13 October, Blackadder flew his final operational patrol with No. 607 Squadron, at Turnhouse, in Hurricane V7223. However, training went on: head-on attacks formed a part of regular training from 15 October onwards—many considered the head-on attack too dangerous due the high closing speeds— and cloud flying and formation also featured in the workload. Blackadder carried out a battle-climb over Dundee with a weather test to break the monotony on 17 October, the only flight he made on this day. On 23 October, he flew out to Drem, the first of four flights made on this day, and the 'Last operational patrol with 607, nothing seen'. He then flew a patrol to Dunbar in Hurricane 'F', then turned south and flew to Usworth. After an overnight stay, he made the return flight to Turnhouse.

Blackadder's arrival back at Turnhouse marked a break with No. 607 Squadron, for he was attached to Turnhouse as a controller (Operations), and back to flying more sedate aircraft—mainly the Hornet Moth W5754, which he mostly flew to Inverness and Grangemouth over the next two days on Group duties. Blackadder now flew less frequently: he did not go up again until 14 November, when he flew to Leuchars with PO Norwood as his passenger and solo back. The reason for this break was simple: after surviving the Battle of France and the Battle of Britain, Blackadder had realised that the war looked set to go on for quite a while yet. It was time, therefore, to think about the future, and to get on with life: Francis Blackadder married Elizabeth Patricia Oswald Kayll ('Paddy'), a cousin of fellow pilot Joe Kayll and a second cousin of Harry Welford. The marriage took place at Sunderland in the afternoon, where Welford had also got married in the morning.

The majority of Blackadder's flights in December were restricted to either the Hornet Moth or the Magister and were of the public relations variety; he twice flew the Magister to Fettes College, Edinburgh, for instance. There were occasional respites from routine for Blackadder, however: one came on 13 December, when, while flying Magister N3934, he 'Beat up the gun posts at Turnhouse'. He also managed to get the odd flight in a Hurricane, for example on 3 December, when he flew P3962 and beat up the gun posts at Drem. This was a No. 607 Squadron Hurricane, which was written off on 20 December, when it crashed on landing at Usworth. The two gun post 'beat ups' were more likely an exercise connected with Blackadder's controller activities than the 'gung ho' manoeuvre of a bored pilot.

Blackadder's last ascents for 1940 were a cross-country flight on 22 December from Turnhouse to Donibristle, Fife, and a local flight to Usworth in Hurricane P2874 on 27 December, presumably for the Christmas leave period. Although he recorded this last one as local, he must have had a good fly-around, because it lasted some fifty minutes—on which no comments appear in his logbook. This was his final flight in Hurricane P2874, otherwise known as 'F'.

1941 began well for Blackadder: he was mentioned in despatches on New Year's Day. There was to be no more flying for him until 1 February, when, although still on controller duties, he made a tour of west Northumberland from his base at Prestwick. He made a trip to Ouston and Usworth on 12 March, probably in connection with the opening of Ouston as a Fighter Sector HQ two days earlier. On 18 March he managed to secure another Hurricane flight, this time the Hurricane P2647, formerly flown with No. 79 Squadron in the Battle of France. It had crashed on the approach to Rouvres airfield, and although repaired it was of no further use in a combat role; nevertheless, it had its uses for training. Blackadder flew it locally for thirty minutes.

For the next two months, Blackadder remained on controller duties at Prestwick and Ayr. His flights were mainly cross-country and in the Magister, as he ferried himself around the various airfields of 13 Fighter Group; Turnhouse, Silloth, West Freugh, and Ouston were among those visited. However, he did fly as a passenger in a Lysander on 30 May—a forty-minute flight from Inverness to Skitten and back. His pilot was his one-time CO and friend from No. 607 Squadron, Jim Vick, now also a controller and with the rank of Wing Commander.

On 1 June came a change; Blackadder was posted to Aldergrove, Northern Ireland, where he took command of the Hurricane-equipped No. 245 Squadron. His first flight was in a No. 602 Squadron Spitfire R7071, and seemed to go well until he indulged in some light aerobatics in an attempt to get a feel for the machine; while attempting a roll, the cockpit hood collapsed, which brought a swift end to his flight. He records that he flew another Spitfire, the R7442, two days later; this aircraft, however, appears to be a Fairey Battle light bomber—the number, although written clearly, must have been a mistake.

From 11 June, Blackadder returned to more familiar ground in flying the Hurricane again. On 15 June, he flew the W9200 on a scramble over Ballyhalbert, and on the 16th, a cross-country flight from Aldergrove to Ouston, by way of Kirkiston. His was the first Hurricane to land.

Blackadder's flying routine took a different turn and began to resemble his flying days with No. 607 Squadron. Cross-country flights were intermixed with the normal duties of a fighter squadron—scrambles and squadron formation flights were back on the agenda, though Blackadder still had the occasional flight in the Magister. With FS Humphries in the passenger seat, he flew a return flight from Limavady, County Londonderry, on 18 June. There were also cross-country flights between Aldergrove and St Angelo, near Enniskillen, with much use of camera-gun operations along the way. Blackadder noted another first when Wg Cdr McGregor made the first Hurricane landing at St Angelo on 20 June.

Throughout the rest of the year Blackadder's flying revolved mainly around the training of a fighter squadron for its move to the south of England. There were camera-gun exercises and cross-country flights mixed with the more mundane convoy patrols and battle climbs, the majority done in either the Hurricane Mk 1 or II. On 27 August, Blackadder departed base for West Freugh in Hurricane II 3470; once there, he switched to a Magister and flew to Ouston; he then returned to West Freugh, where he picked up his Hurricane again. He continued his journey to Drem and Turnhouse, before moving on to Tern Hill and Colerne, then flew the reverse course back to base, where he arrived on 29 August.

On 2 September, Blackadder flew Hurricane Z3311 'H' on a convoy patrol from Middle Wallop, and recorded, 'W.F.B. and Kruta (Czech pilot) carry out first convoy patrol in the south 15 miles SSW Swanage'. The squadron then moved onto offensive patrols and night flying across France, such as on 7 September, on which Blackadder wrote, 'AA fire seen over Boulogne raided by the RAF'. On 8 September, Blackadder logs an account of leading No. 245 Squadron's feint attack on Cherbourg as part of a main sweep; he gives the entry the heading, 'Scramble'.

Always keen to add new types of aircraft to the list in his logbook, Blackadder flew in Havoc AX914 on 22 October on a night flying test; he was, however, only a passenger—the pilot was Sqn Ldr Kelly. In the last months of 1941, the squadron may have been back to the routine training programme, but Blackadder still found time to fit in the Magister. A highpoint of the year came on 13 November, when Air Commodore HRH the Duke of Kent made a visit to the squadron.

Blackadder now entered a lengthy break from flying. His days with No. 245 Squadron came to a close when, on 13 July 1942, he was posted back to controlling duties for 10 Group at Rudloe Manor. This was succeeded by a course at the Army Staff College, followed by a posting to HQ Fighter Command as a Wing Commander (Tactics), before the move on to HQ Allied Expeditionary Forces on 28 September 1943.

1945 opened with the award of the OBE on 1 January. Blackadder then returned to flying duties by taking command of the Air Fighting Development Unit at Wittering. He also took on a number of new, as well as familiar, types, flying Spitfires and Hurricanes, and Mustangs and Tempests alike. On 21 February, he flew Spitfire Mk XXI SM356 up to 22,500 feet. At the other end of the scale, he flew Auster LB332 solo for 'experience on the type'.

Most of Blackadder's flights during this period were in the various marks of the Spitfire. However, he did manage to squeeze in a flight in other aircraft: the Moth Minor, on 10 March, again for 'experience on type'. The following day, he flew a Tempest II on speed runs at 11,500 feet, and on 14 March, flew as passenger in a Mosquito RS554. This was part of a four-day tour of France and the Netherlands which included visits to Reims, Asch, and Schijndel; Blackadder made the return flight from Schijndel in a Spitfire.

On 3 April, Blackadder flew a Tiger Cat, a ship-borne night fighter; this he recorded as a 'handling flight'. He faced a bit of a change with his next flight, which ushered him into the jet-age for the first time: this was a handling flight on the Gloster Meteor III EE243, on 2 April. On 7 April, he flew again in the same Meteor, carrying out handling trials at 18,000 feet. One of the more unusual aircraft he flew was the Me 109 G14, coded EA2, on 22 April; although a later model than those he had encountered in combat, it was basically similar. On 25 April, he flew a P47 Thunderbolt as a test for rocket projectiles; things did not go well, as the single diary entry, 'failure', indicates. No further comments elucidate what kind of failure it might have occurred.

On 8 May, Blackadder boldly wrote the legend, 'Hostilities ceased in Europe at 00.01 hours'. This was also meant to signal a gap in his flying, which began again on 11 May, once more in one of his old adversaries—on this occasion, the Me 110, coded EA 4. This was a handling flight which he made no comments about, though it must have made him reminiscent of France. He flew the Me 110 solo, even though it was a two-seat aircraft. For the rest of the month he reverted once more to flying various marks of the Spitfire, many of which were still in front-line RAF service.

On 23 May, he flew the Spitfire Mk 21 LA218 and noted that it was 'the contra propeller version'. Although Blackadder made no comments on this aircraft in his logbook, other pilots did, which caused more than a few waves to pass through the upper echelons of the RAF. For Jeffrey Quill, the Spitfire Mk 21was an effective fighting machine, though he conceded, 'The pilots of the A&AEE and the Air Fighting Development Unit thought otherwise'. Quill placed much confidence in the younger pilots, unlike the Air Fighting Development Unit; Quill originally disapproved of their favour towards older pilots, and thought that their decision not to continue with the Spitfire Mk 21 was 'An ill-judged and premature decision'.[10]

Blackadder, third from the right, at Ouston.

The Air Fighting Development Unit later stated in an early report that development of the Spitfire Mk 21 should cease; work on it carried on, however, after handling problems were carried out. Though it remained controversial, the Spitfire Mk 21 was eventually flown in RAF service.

For Blackadder made more flights on the Meteor III. Among his tests were gun-firing trials, carried out at 29,600 feet on 15 May, and measured take-offs, on 22 May. However, his days with the Air Fighting Development Unit were coming to an end, along with his RAF service. On 25 May, he recorded his last flight with the unit when he flew Spitfire RS525 on a return flight to Colerne. In November 1945, Blackadder finally left RAF service.

After leaving the RAF, Blackadder returned to his civilian employment with the Runciman Shipping Company based in Newcastle, and continued to live in County Durham. His flying days had seemed to come to an end when, in 1946, the AAF and No. 607 Squadron were reborn—on paper, at

Summer camp at Lübeck: Blackadder is seated fourth from the left.

least. Many who had survived the war returned to a modernised No. 607 Squadron; among the 'old hands' was Blackadder, who, according to the squadron records, rejoined his old squadron in September 1946. He was gazetted as a Flight Lieutenant on 5 December.

Blackadder did not fly again until 19 October 1946. He flew as a passenger aboard the Harvard KF313 from Ouston, the new post-war home of No. 607 Squadron; this was also the first aircraft on the newly formed No. 607 Squadron. This was a cross-country flight from Ouston to West Raynham piloted by Flt Lt McConnell—the squadron training officer at the time—and the return leg was flown the following day.

Like in the pre-war days, it took quite an amount of time for pilots to progress from one area of training to the next, due to employment commitments—and so it was with Blackadder. His first solo was not to be until 24 November; once again, it was in the Harvard, on this occasion the FX280. Although he flew the Harvard several times, mostly locally, it was on 12 January 1947 that his big day arrived: having done a local flight in the Harvard, he then did a local flight in Spitfire XIV TZ116— Blackadder once more had a fighter's wings beneath him. Unfortunately, he left no comments in his logbook on what must have been an uplifting event.

Blackadder only flew four more times in January 1947, and not at all the following month. He fared little better in March, flying only once in a Harvard with PO Tony Dunford, also a training officer, in the passenger seat. The month of April was free of any flying at all, and Blackadder only made another flight, local and of thirty minutes, in Spitfire AH794 on 10 May. A further flight, local and lasting one hour, came on 17 May, in Spitfire SM929. His final flight of the month came on 24 May, when he flew up to Turnhouse in Spitfire NH658, and made a return flight to Ouston later in the day.

Blackadder's flying hours increased in June. He carried out a forty-five minute formation flight on 6 June, and followed this up with a local flight in the Harvard with Fg Off. Thompson in the passenger seat. On 21 and 22 June, he flew Spitfire T2 178 to Tangmere, making an overnight stay and returning the following day to Ouston. On 29 June, he again carried out two flights; a weather test followed by a formation flight with Jim Bazin and Tony Dunford.

July 1947 brought back memories of the olden days, as the squadron embarked on its first post-war annual summer camp. This year, it was held at Leuchars, beginning on the 20th. Blackadder did not arrive with them the squadron, again probably due to work commitments, but came a day or so later, since he recorded a formation flight with Jim Bazin and Tony Dunford on 22 July. It was from this flight onwards that

No. 607 Squadron at Ouston. Blackadder is seated seventh from the left in the second row.

Spitfire 'D' at Ouston.

Blackadder showing some locals around a Tiger Moth, probably in Ouston, using his connection with the Durham University Air Squadron.

Blackadder began to use the aircraft individual code letter—rather than its number—again; the flight was made in Spitfire RAN, 'F'. Although this flight was in 'F', it did not become his personal aircraft, because he appears only to have flown it once. The following day, he flew Spitfire 'K' for an hour, to 'Inspect Naval Review': the occasion was the Naval Review on the River Clyde, attended by HRH King George VI and Queen Elizabeth, and other members of the royal family. Blackadder ended the month's flying with a return cross-country flight from Leuchars to Ouston in Spitfire 'D'. He did not return from summer camp to Ouston with the rest of the squadron to Ouston on 2 August, but may have stayed in Scotland.

In August, Blackadder flew only once, in a formation flight of forty-five minutes' duration on the 23rd. He did not fly again until 6 September, in Spitfire 'M', when he left Ouston for Turnhouse and then flew across to Dyce; both flights were of some thirty minutes' duration. He then went southwards back to Ouston, giving no explanation for this flight in his logbook. On 13 September, Blackadder flew a formation flight with Jim Bazin, then on 20 September a squadron formation, again uncommented upon in his logbook. Jim Bazin also gives no further information, but merely states, 'Formation flight' for the 13th, and like Blackadder,

'Squadron formation' for the 20th. Blackadder flew Spitfire 'M' on both flights.[11]

On 26 October, Blackadder flew Spitfire 'P' on a thirty-five minute flight that he noted was an 'acceptance test'. Presumably this was a new aircraft on the squadron, and Blackadder was giving it a 'shake-down'. He carried out a local flight from Ouston on 29 October in Spitfire 'E', and the following day took off from Ouston on a cross-country flight destined for RAF Honiley in Warwickshire. However, he fell short of the mark and was forced to land at Yeadon; no further comments appear in his logbook for this flight. Later the same day, he was flown back to Ouston by Flt Lt Buddin in a Harvard.

Blackadder's logbook shows only one flight for 1948. This took place on 4 November, when he flew Spitfire 'M' on an air test. This was to be Blackadder's final recorded flight. It was also this year that he became the squadron adjutant, and that No. 607 Squadron held its first overseas annual summer camp; the airfield was Lübeck, in Germany, a favourite with the pilots because of its proximity to the coast. The group photograph features Blackadder. As the one flight he recorded in 1948 was not made during the summer camp period, it is not known how he got there, or back again. He made no recorded flight during his stay.

With the end of 1948 came the end of Blackadder's flying career. He

Squadron reunion: Kayll, ??, and Blackadder (from left to right).

was gazetted in the 31 May edition of *The London Gazette*: Secretarial Branch, transfer to reserve (class A), and transfer to another branch.

> Flight Lieutenant W. F. Blackadder, O.B.E., DSO. (90282) to the reserve (class A) and transferred t the General Duties Branch retaining his rank, 22nd December 1948.

This did not mean that Blackadder's ties the RAF were totally cut. On 26 July 1948, he became CO of the Northumberland Wing of the ATC (Air Traffic Control). He retained this post until on 27 November 1950, when he retired, it is likely, due to the ever increasing work load at the shipping line. His final resignation was announced in *The London Gazette* on 16 March 1951, under 'commission resigned as from 27 November 1950'.

After acquiring the Anchor line in 1965, the Runciman Line was merged with the Anchor Line. Now a bigger shipping line, it had outgrown its Tyneside base, and to make the business more viable, moved to one of the larger centres of the shipping industry—Glasgow. The story of Blackadder, and his move, was picked up by the local press, for instance the *Newcastle Journal*. It cited Blackadder as having said, 'The dice of local commerce are loaded heavily against the smaller men and the future must surely lie in amalgamation of the bigger units'. The same newspaper mentioned Blackadder's war-time service in the RAF, his DSO award, and that he was 'A retiring man by nature'.[12]

Blackadder had been president of the North-East Coast Institute of Engineers and Shipbuilders since 1964, and was due to leave the position in November 1966. According to the press, Blackadder had bridged the gap between British ship-owners and the shipbuilders during his time in the post, thus strengthening their industries against fast-growing international competition. This work not only helped the shipping industry, but also the spin-off industries along Tyneside.

Newcastle University also paid tribute to Blackadder. Between 1966 and 1987, the university held lectures on the shipping industry which were transformed into an annual event known as the 'Blackadder Lecture'. In more recent years, the practise of the annual lecture appears to have become less frequent, coming to an end in 1987. Now, sadly, it appears to have disappeared altogether.

Blackadder spent the next ten years—the last of his working life—in Stewarton, Ayrshire. He retired from his post as Vice Chairman of the Anchor Line in 1978, and shortly thereafter moved his family back to his adoptive home in County Durham, to the village of Heighington. Although he was Scottish by birth, he had spent most of his life in County Durham, and—although he had played rugby for Scotland—had also

Above left: Wooden plaque commemorating the decorated at Usworth.

Above right: Blackadder after the war.

Blackadder's
gravestone.

been a keen follower of the Northern League RFC, making many friends and connections there. Fellow pilot Bobbie Pumphrey was one who had been introduced to rugby and to the AAF team by Blackadder, who had captained the Northern League RFC side from 1937 to 1939. In the post-war years, he had spent much of his time with the Northern League, and presided over it from 1953 to 1954.

In tandem with his long association with No. 607 Squadron and the Runciman shipping lines, Blackadder had found time to carry out his duty as a JP. Illness eventually caught up with him, and he died and was cremated at Darlington in November 1997. In 2006, his family had two memorials erected in the family home in Berwickshire. One was on a gravestone in Chirnside, a sandstone headstone carrying his name, the dates of birth and death, and beneath them the legend, 'ONE OF THE "FEW" IN THE BATTLE OF BRITAIN'. The second memorial is in Edrom, near Duns, and is smaller and carved from marble; the inscription is the same. William Francis Blackadder—former pilot, international rugby player, and shipping line chairman—had come home to his family roots.

Endnotes

1 Beginnings

1. Interview of Jen Main, Archivist, Merchiston Castle School, Edinburgh.
2. No. 607 Squadron Operational Readiness Book (ORB), The National Archives.
3. Runciman Papers, Robinson Library, Newcastle University, WR ADD B/5
4. *Ibid*.
5. *Ibid*.
6. *Ibid*.
7. RAF Historical Branch.
8. Charles Edward English flew through much of the Battle of Britain as a pilot with No. 85 Squadron, during which he often flew as wingman to the squadron CO Peter Townsend. He was later posted to No. 605 (County of Warwick) Squadron. He was killed in action with this squadron on 7 October 1940. He is buried in St Andrews and Jesmond Cemetery, Newcastle upon Tyne.
9. Runciman Papers, correspondence with Leigh Mallory.
10. Upon leaving an AAF Squadron, normal practice was to resign entirely or join another auxiliary squadron in the area you were moving to.
11. Logbooks of Group Captain William Nigel Henry Turner.
12. Runciman Papers.
13. *Ibid.*, correspondence with Lord Londonderry.
14. Logbooks of Flt Lt George Dudley Craig.
15. Logbooks of Wing Commander James Michael Bazin.

16. Runciman Papers, correspondence with Leigh Mallory.
17. *Ibid*.

5 Post France

1. Peter Anthony Burnell-Philips had originally been a Cranwell cadet and an officer in the RAF. Shortly before the war he was forced to resign his commission as the result of a low-flying demeanour. He was later to regain officer status shortly before his death 9 February 1941.
2. Welford, Harry, *The Unrelenting Years. 1916–1946* (Newton, 1997), p. 112.
3. *Ibid*., p. 108.
4. Although much of the literature on the Battle of Britain and the local press predicted that the Luftwaffe would bomb various targets in the North East, the only target on the Luftwaffe's plans for that region was Driffield. Usworth was never a target.
5. Personal communication with the late William Hubert Rigby Whitty.
6. Jim Bazin was flying Hurricane P3668 that day. His only statement is 'operational'. The following day he was flying Hurricane P2617, its only known fight in the battle. His family have shared with the author that he hit his face on the gun sight in the forced landing.
7. Logbook of Francis Blackadder.
8. Air Vice-Marshal Johnstone, Sandy, *Spitfire Into War* (London: Grafton Books, 1988), p. 182.
9. Logbook of Jim Bazin.
10. Quill, Jeffrey, *Spitfire. A Test Pilot's Story* (London: John Murray, 1983), p. 274.
11. Logbook of Jim Bazin.
12. *Newcastle Journal*, 9 May 1966.